A Man, A Plan, (yet lacking) a Canal — Panama

L.L. Donahue

A Man, A Plan, (yet lacking) a Canal—Panama
Linda L. Donahue
Copyright Linda L. Donahue 2007
Published by Yard Dog Press at Kindle

ISBN 978-1-945941-38-2

This is a work of fiction. All the characters and events portrayed in this book are fictitious, and any resemblance to real people is purely coincidental.

First Edition Copyright © 2007 by Linda L. Donahue
Second Edition Copyright © 2023 by Linda L. Donahue

All rights reserved. No part of this book may be reproduced in any form or by any electronic or mechanical means, including information storage and retrieval systems, without permission in writing from the publisher, except by a reviewer, who may quote brief passages in a review. Any members of educational institutions wishing to photocopy part or all of the work for classroom use, or publishers who would like to obtain permission to include the work in an anthology should send their inquiries to Yard Dog Press at the address below.

Yard Dog Press
710 W. Redbud Lane
Alma, AR 72921-7247

http://www.yarddogpress.com

Edited by Selina Rosen
Technical Editor Lynn Rosen
Cover art by John Kevin Hopkins

First Edition March 1, 2007
Second Edition June 15, 2023
Printed in the United States of America
0 9 8 7 6 5 4 3 2

Table of Contents

Table of Contents iii
Chapter One 1
Chapter Two 7
Chapter Three 23
Chapter Four 35
Chapter Five 45
Chapter Six 51
Chapter Seven 55
End Note: 61
About the Author v
About the Cover Artist vii
Yard Dog Press Titles as of this Publication Date: ix

L.L. Donahue

Chapter One
The Plan

December 1670

Captain Henry Morgan squatted on a moonlit beach before the officers of his newly assembled fleet. "Gentlemen. Never have such forces come together."

Thirty-seven ships harbored at Cabo Tiburon off the western tip of Hispaniola. Morgan's own flagship, the most heavily armed, boasted twenty-two cannons and six brass swivel guns.

"We are invincible," Morgan said.

A round of cheers stirred up screeches and squawks from the dark jungle behind them. Amid the cawing cries, Morgan swore he heard his name. Soon, all the world would know of him as the greatest privateer of the 17th century.

"To that end, gents, let this one word inspire you." Firelight glinted off the emerald rosette ring on Morgan's index finger. The ring was a gift from Don Juan Pérez de Guzmán, president of Panama, making this a fitting time to wear it. Leaning into the gathered circle, Morgan said, "*Panama.*"

Cold silence enveloped the gathering of battle-scarred pirates. Their faces, bronzed by the guttering light from oil lanterns, took on a cowardly, yellow hue. Then, rippling outward like an echo, the officers of Morgan's War Council repeated, "Panama City?"

"Impossible," and "We'll be killed," was murmured among the ranks. Some men lacked imagination, while fear limited others.

The first familiar face to catch Morgan's eye was Captain Edward Collier. Though a man of some caution, Collier was no coward.

"Have you some intelligence we haven't?" Collier asked.

"*Et*, has Pérez de Guzmán been summoned *en Espagne*?" Antony du Puis, a buccaneer captain, asked in a heavy French accent.

Reputedly, the best trained forces in the Spanish New World served under Don Juan Pérez de Guzmán. Yet, even peasant

A Man, A Plan, (yet lacking) A Canal—Panama

volunteers were an improvement over typical Spanish soldiers who were more often than not conscripts or convicts.

Morgan stroked the tuft of hair on his chin. "To my knowledge, Don Pérez de Guzmán is still president." Although it'd been two years since their last correspondence.

"Then I repeat my question," Collier said. "What do you know that we don't?"

Louder concerns arose. Dissenting voices blended into indistinguishable, cowardly muttering. Morgan's scowl cowed everyone ... except Collier.

"A lofty goal, Henry, to be certain. But how can we breach Panama City's fortifications, assuming we can even reach it?"

The outspoken du Puis spoke up next, waving his arms for emphasis. "Why risk it when we can more easily raid the coast?" Other officers nodded, further emboldening the buccaneer captain. "Call for a vote, *Capitaine* Morgan. They will agree *avec moi*."

Morgan unfurled a map and weighed its corners with handfuls of pebbles and beach. "For the moment, gentlemen, let's consider Captain du Puis's proposal and assume highly successful raids on Cartagena and Vera Cruz." As Morgan pointed out the coastal cities, his finger left behind a speckled trail of sand. "What would those raids yield altogether? Now think how thin that booty would spread among our combined crews."

The assembled fleet carried two thousand well-armed men, each entitled to a share.

"Something to divvy is better than nothing," Collier said.

"*C'est vrai.* I say we vote," du Puis said.

Consenting mumbles agreed. To silence them, Morgan struck the map with his fist, driving it partway into the sand.

"Panama City is the wealthiest of Spain's holdings." Morgan locked gazes with Collier. If he won him over, the rest would follow, including that French parrot, du Puis. "If half the rumors are true, we'll *all* be filthy rich."

Collier folded his arms. "Panama City can't be taken."

"For argument's sake, say it can. Consider the prize." When Morgan tapped the elegantly scrolled "Panama City" across the map, his ring caught the lantern light. Like an asteriated sapphire, the largest emerald flashed a green-fire star burst.

The star burst momentarily mesmerized Morgan,

L.L. Donahue

transporting his thoughts back to Port Royal. After meeting with Governor Modyford, Morgan had run across a near-toothless hag with a cloudy eye. She'd grabbed Morgan's hand, saying, "Your ring is a harbinger of fate. It promises great fame and great tragedy. It leads to places unknown—though perhaps, captain, those places are best left undiscovered." Morgan had shaken off her hold, insisting she was mad. Then as he'd walked away, she called out, her withered voice startlingly clear, "Beware of angry gods who covet the eyes of the goddess. Do not set foot on their soil."

Morgan shivered, driving away the eerie woman's prophesy. He was a man of reason, not a superstitious fool as were most pirates and sailors.

"Henry? You were saying?"

Morgan met Collier's gaze. "Damnation, man, consider the possibility."

"I have." With his finger, Collier drew a line across the isthmus from the Caribbean coast to the Pacific. "No one has ever attempted such a deep, inland raid, and through a jungle no less. So I'll ask again, what makes you certain you'll succeed?"

"My past success convinces me. Haven't you heard of my latest encounter with Spain's forces?"

Morgan paced. Movement always enhanced a great tale, especially one spreading his own fame. As well, patrolling the beach gave him the opportunity to assess the assembled officers. A good hard look was often enough to judge a man's fortitude and make a bond.

"We were blockaded in the Bay of Maricaibo," Morgan began, "having successfully sacked Maricaibo City. Three Spanish men-of-war attacked, their largest warship carrying forty guns to the fourteen of my heaviest armed ship. We were out-manned and out-gunned, yet we prevailed."

Captain John Galoone laughed. "Aren't we always?"

"Aye, that's the truth," Morgan said with a grin. "We've all run up against greater odds and, more often than not, succeeded. Yea, Panama City will be a challenge. One we'll win." He waved towards the bay at an assembled fleet so large that only a portion was visible. "We have numbers on our side."

A consensus of murmurs meekly agreed. Even Antony du Puis nodded. But Collier just studied the map.

A Man, A Plan, (yet lacking) A Canal—Panama

Morgan raised a fist, his thumb absently rubbing the emerald ring. "Swear me your loyalty and I'll repay you in more gold and silver and priceless gems than your ship's hold can carry."

"There's still the jungle to consider," Collier said.

Captain Joseph Brodely pushed through the crowd. "If I might interject a suggestion?" Beneath his quiet demeanor resided a determined man, driven by strength of will. Morgan had often said that Brodely would keep fighting two days after his death, being too stubborn to lie down.

"By all means, Joseph, speak up," Morgan said.

"We'll need a guide. I suggest we raid the Isle of St. Catharine."

The Spanish sent numerous "felons" to that island—many of them former slaves and Indian natives. Any of them would make a willing guide, if only to revenge themselves against their Spanish masters.

"It makes strategic sense," Galoone added. "We'll need a safe harbor."

Collier grinned. "I like it. There's a perverse pleasure in taking back what was once England's."

"I concur," du Puis said. "With a base behind and a guide to lead us, this plan may not be so mad after all."

Morgan raised his arms and shouted, "How say you all? Shall it be the City of Panama by way of St. Catharine's Isle?"

"Aye!" the War Council shouted.

From the jungle's depths, night birds squawked in agitation. Leaves and fronds rustled amid the sound of hundreds of bird wings beating the air.

"As we are agreed, let us draw up the articles."

"I nominate Henry Morgan for admiral," Collier said.

"I second," Brodely said. "Seeing as it's his venture." He grinned at Morgan. "We know you'll take the credit, so you may as well take any blame that comes of it."

The vote was, of course, unanimous; that bit being merely for formality. Nonetheless, Morgan accepted the position with a gracious bow.

The War Council then voted to pay Morgan one-hundredth of the proceeds. Though a seemingly meager share for an admiral of so great a fleet, Morgan expected the raid would yield unheard of wealth. Additionally, for the use of their ships,

L.L. Donahue

captains would receive what constituted eight men's shares. Surgeons were voted an extra two hundred pieces of eight for medical supplies, and carpenters an additional one hundred.

For two days, Morgan and his council palavered over details. Only the actual doling out of rewards and compensations took longer. As was common practice, those funds were drawn from the accumulated booty before divvying what remained into shares.

Among the hundred-some compensations proposed for mutilations were: Loss of a limb should pay out the equivalent of six hundred pieces of eight or six slaves, with more than double paid for losing two limbs. An eye or finger was valued at one hundred or one slave, while being blinded garnered a greater compensation. Every pirate knew of at least one Brethren of the Coast who'd been reduced to begging and none wished to end their careers in so ignominious a manner. T'was a better fate to be hanged.

An English captain waved his stump. "What about us who've only the one hand to lose?"

Morgan growled. At this rate, they'd still be writing the articles come the new year. "We'll none be paying for what you lost on a past venture."

Scowling, the English captain, nonetheless, relented. "I suppose them's fair amounts seeing as I didn't receive half that much for me original loss."

"Then we're agreed." Morgan dipped the quill in ink, preferring the document to be penned in his own hand.

"As for rewards," Morgan continued, "I say the first to run up Britain's flag earns fifty pieces of eight." He was, after all, a privateer in the service of Charles II and possessed the Letters of Marque to prove it. "Is that agreeable?"

A cheer answered, instantly raising morale.

In the end, the rewards included: Collecting useful intelligence earned an extra two hundred. Grenadiers received five pieces of eight for every grenade landing inside fortress walls. And a prize of one thousand pieces of eight would be awarded for capturing a Spanish vessel.

"With one stipulation," Morgan said. "Boarding a ship of any other nation shall be considered treasonous and those involved shall be dealt with accordingly. This, gentlemen, is nonnegotiable."

A Man, A Plan, (yet lacking) A Canal—Panama

Amid grousing, a general agreement arose. And finally, before Morgan lost all patience, the articles were completed then signed. As a clergyman would say, a devil's pact had been made. To Morgan, it marked the beginning of his greatest enterprise.

During their last night harbored at Cabo Tiburon, Morgan shared wine with Collier, Brodely, and Galoone aboard the fleet's flagship. Raising his glass, Morgan toasted, "To your new appointments, gentlemen."

Morgan's first act as admiral was to promote many of his captains. Among them, Collier and Brodely were now vice-admirals and Galoone a rear-admiral. Even so, the crews, Morgan's included, would likely call them captain out of habit.

His second act as admiral was to issue commissions to the various ships, giving their captains the right to capture Spanish vessels, at sea or in harbor, according to the right of reprisals. These commissions, on behalf of the crown of England, condoned any act of violence against the enemy.

England and Spain were at war. Whether called pirates, buccaneers or privateers, Morgan and his crew expected to receive no less from the enemy.

Collier raised his glass. "Not a bad wine, Henry. There's hardly any dregs." Then he toasted, "For England."

"To success," Brodely added.

"And wealth," Galoone finished. "Never forget the wealth."

Morgan held his glass aloft. "To Don Juan Pérez de Guzmán, without whom this venture would never have been conceived."

Aboard every ship, the crew celebrated pirate-fashion, with drunken revelry and gunfire. Hearing a cannon blast, Morgan tensed. The glass stem cracked in his grasp. Recalling an incident on the Isle de la Vaca that had cost him a good ship, the *Oxford*, he started towards the cabin door.

"Let them celebrate, Henry," Brodely said.

"You've already cautioned the ships' captains," Collier said. "You'll undermine their authority if you don't trust them to keep their crews in line."

Reluctantly, Morgan grabbed another glass and poured himself more wine. "You say that now. Wait until your ship explodes and you fight your way past burning timbers and fling yourself overboard."

Brodely laughed. "At least it's not far to shore."

L.L. Donahue

Chapter Two
The Isle of St. Catharine

After four days at sea, the mountainous Isle of St. Catharine loomed on the horizon. Morgan dispatched a fast sailing ship mounting fourteen guns to blockade the port while the rest of the fleet dropped anchor.

Morgan took a thousand men, half his forces, ashore. Divided into eight squadrons, they marched through the woods, led by scouts who had ransacked St. Catharine Isle years ago under Captain Mansvelt's command.

When one of the scouts ran back, Morgan called a halt.

Gaspar doubled over, catching his breath. Rumor had it he'd served under Mansvelt *and* L'Olonnais. Having survived L'Olonnais's known cruelty was noteworthy in itself. Gaspar doffed his woolen cap. For a buccaneer, he spoke with hardly a trace of an accent. Rasping, he said in ragged bursts, "We've been talking, captain, and we're fairly certain the Platforma St. Jago lies beyond those trees. As best we recall, the battery has four cannons."

"Only four?" Feeling a bit jaunty over the good news, Morgan called together his squadron leaders. "Tonight we feast in the governor's mansion."

After the squadrons were in position, Morgan fired a single shot. His pirate crew charged, firing their pistols.

Yet no shots were returned. Indentations in the ground were the only proof that cannons once stood there. Beyond the deserted battery, the village and the governor's house had already been ransacked by fleeing Spaniards.

Standing in the middle of a deserted road, Morgan tucked his pistols into his sash. "Scouts! Search the island. Don't return until you've found the governor's fort or a farm worth raiding."

Before long, the buccaneer scouts returned with news of a fort on the other side of the small island.

The squadrons marched through sparse woods, past a rocky rise, and beyond an open field to reach the far shoreline. A

A Man, A Plan, (yet lacking) A Canal—Panama

Spanish fortress perched atop a lesser island, one not on the charts. A bridge spanned the turquoise waters separating that spit of land from St. Catharine. Atop the fortress perched smaller forts, fortified strongpoints with cannons and swivel guns. Batteries circled the walls to defend the lesser island.

Again Morgan assembled his leaders. "Any suggestions?"

Collier uttered his usual sentiments. "It appears impregnable."

At times Collier was too cautious. Yet he only hesitated before a battle, never during. Once the man committed, Morgan trusted him to see a fight to the end.

Nevertheless, Morgan needled the man. "Edward, have you always planned for failure?"

"Only lately, Henry."

Brodely squinted at the fortress. "I say we charge the bridge. It's the only way across,"

Not a canoe was in sight. Indeed, the only viable means across was by bridge or by swimming—and the latter held no appeal.

"You're both mad," Collier said. "I say attack by ship."

Brodely scowled. "The water is too shallow. Even supposing we could maneuver the sloops without beaching them, they aren't armed heavily enough to take that fortress. Either we charge or we turn tail like whipped dogs. Which is it to be?"

No one had more guts than Joseph Brodely. However, being superior marksmen, buccaneers stood the best chance of getting across. Therefore Morgan laid a hand on du Puis's shoulder. "Your squadron leads."

"I should lead," Brodely groused.

Morgan met Brodely's disappointed glare. "You can lead the second assault."

John Galoone muttered, "Assuming there is one. As I recall, moats are highly defensible."

"They can still be crossed," Brodely said with conviction.

The squadron leaders readied their forces.

Du Puis fired a shot, sounding the first charge. Buccaneers swarmed the field, firing as they ran.

Gunfire exploded from a corner fort perched atop the walls. Cannons fired from the battery directly below, belching sulfurous smoke. From the next two nearest forts, Spanish soldiers cried, "¡Perros ingleses! ¡Enemigos de dios y del rey!"

L.L. Donahue

English dogs! Enemies of God and king!

Under a barrage of grapeshot, the buccaneers retreated. Of those hit, only two fell dead. Several more had shot dug from their hides and the wounds either stitched or seared. Apparently, stage one of the plan wouldn't go so easily.

Morgan shoved his pistols into his sash. Galoone was right about the moat, but that didn't mean the fortress couldn't be taken. Morgan had faced worse odds and succeeded.

Brodely approached. "Orders, captain?"

"Tell me your thoughts, Joseph."

Brodely stared across the grassy field. "There's no cover and no sneaking across at night." He pointed at the torches rimming the fortress walls. "While we're sitting on our arses working out a plan, I suspect they'll be preparing an armed reception."

Reluctantly, Morgan agreed. The Spaniards had every advantage, from shooting down on Morgan's crew to waiting them out.

"We aren't giving up, are we," Brodely said, not asked.

Neither patience nor direct force would work. Morgan clapped Brodely's back. "We need a plan."

They made camp at the deserted battery. Because Spaniards had pulled down the storehouse's thatched roof, the woods offered the only meager shelter. Lacking any comforts and their empty bellies aching, Morgan's crew grumbled themselves to sleep.

Morgan, however, was wide awake. His ship's surgeon, Exquemelin, along with Collier and Brodely kept Morgan company beside a popping fire. Meanwhile, John Galoone and his men made the rounds—in case any Spaniards were foolish enough to leave the fortress.

"It'll be strategy that wins this one," Morgan said.

"Aye," Collier mused. "Something they'd never expect."

For hours, they stared at the sputtering fire. Sometimes Brodely mumbled something then shook his head, discarding the almost spoken idea. Collier paced while Morgan's gaze wandered deeper into the dying flames. The fire conjured visions of the fire-boat he'd used to break the blockade at Maricaibo Bay. Unfortunately, that tactic wouldn't work here.

"Lady Luck has deserted us," Brodely said.

Collier looked up. "As are the stars."

"How's that?" Even as Morgan asked the question, he spied

A Man, A Plan, (yet lacking) A Canal—Panama

the dense cloud bank rolling in from the sea.

Black, writhing clouds blotted out the stars. Rainfall burst from the skies. Cold, needle-sharp rain woke the slumbering crew. Amid renewed grumbles of hunger were added complaints of being cold and wet.

Morgan was quietly thankful for his wool coat and boots. He even spared a bit of pity for those pirates lacking either. Yet had they spent past gains wiser, they wouldn't be in misery now. Plan ahead had always been Morgan's motto.

Ironically, it was just that, a good plan, that he lacked.

The downpour settled into a miserable mist. Anything that could still burn was burned. The already ruined supply huts became the makings of struggling bonfires that the crew huddled around to reclaim some sleep.

In the ensuing quiet, Morgan resumed his thoughts.

Gaspar dragged more bramble for Morgan's campfire. Rain had stretched his woolen cap so it hung past his ears.

Brodely invited Gaspar to sit. "Was the island this miserable when you raided it under Mansvelt? Because you could have warned us, mate."

"I expect the mind fades over the years," Collier teased, his mouth curling slightly at the corners, hinting at a grin.

"Pah." Gaspar stoked the fire with a stick. "*Non*, Captain Brodely, this is not how I remember it. It wasn't winter then."

"As I recall," Brodely added, "it wasn't the same as you remembered in Maracaibo either."

Collier ticked the count on his fingers. "The Spaniards erected three new batteries, another strongpoint, and, let us not forget the bog. How could you forget a bog?"

Exquemelin took the branch from Gaspar and thrust it into the fire. Another Frenchmen, Exquemelin, like Gaspar, spoke with only a slight accent. "If you'd served under L'Olonnais as we had, your memory might also suffer."

After leaving L'Olonnais's service, Exquemelin hadn't smiled for a year. Until recently, he'd been as apprehensive as a fox in a roomful of hounds.

Hearing the buccaneer devil's name, Gaspar blanched and crossed himself. "*Sacre Dieu*."

"I understand you were with him in the end," Brodely said.

"*Oui*," Gaspar said. "Wild savages set upon us. They hacked *Capitaine* L'Olonnais to pieces and burned him limb by limb. I

L.L. Donahue

thank God I escaped before they did the same to me."

Exquemelin, who seldom spoke an ill-word of anyone, said quietly, "Never did a more wretched man receive a more just fate."

"Well now, there's a cheery tale for the campfire," Collier said. "What say we next discuss the punishment for piracy?"

"Unless we capture that fort," Brodely said, "won't any of us be charged with piracy."

"A Trojan Horse would be useful about now," Collier said.

Brodely grunted. "Unless it comes mounted with cannons, I don't see what good it'd do."

Morgan wished he'd brought a deck of cards. Gambling quickened the mind—as did a good stout ale. Reconsidering, he wished he'd brought the ale.

"Bloody weather." Morgan drew his coat tighter and leaned towards Exquemelin. "I hope, surgeon, you're as good with ague as you are with the needle."

Exquemelin shrugged. "There's not much call for curing ague. Mostly you outlast it or it outlasts you. But if we'd thought ahead, we'd brought rum to stave off the chill and sickness."

Morgan laughed hard. "You, sir, are a prince among surgeons. Right about now, I'd trade a ship for a warmed rum."

Exquemelin shivered then held his palms towards the fire. "Aye, captain. Under the circumstances, we could make better use of a case of spirits than the bullets and powder we have. Do you suppose the Spaniards will consider a trade?"

By daybreak, the cursed mist eased off. Sunlight broke through thinning clouds. Though the December day was still cold, the crew stripped to their skivvies and laid out their clothing and boots to dry, Singing the same old complaints, they took great pains to dry out their guns and powder.

Morgan and Exquemelin paced, digging parallel trenches in the rain-soaked ground. "How are the wounded?" Morgan asked.

"They'll live. Most were only grazed. One man will probably lose the use of his left hand—though he needn't." At Morgan's raised eyebrow, Exquemelin explained, "They never follow my instructions, captain. Never clean their wounds or change the dressing. Never."

"Ah, well, it's his hand," Morgan said.

A Man, A Plan, (yet lacking) A Canal—Panama

"We're lucky only two died. Perhaps we should quit this island before your luck runs out," Exquemelin said.

Morgan glowered at the Frenchman. "I daresay you never made such a suggestion to your last captain."

Exquemelin blanched and shook his head. "Few ever disagreed with Françoise L'Olonnais and lived."

"Then don't be telling me my business." Morgan swallowed a growl, not intending to be sharp. Exquemelin simply didn't have enough sand in his blood to be a good privateer.

Brodely strolled towards them, tying the cuffs of his nearly-dried sleeves. "Morning, captain, and a good one at that, seeing as the Spaniards are ignoring us."

Throughout the woods, taking advantage of sunny patches, nearly a thousand men spread out gunpowder to dry. A hundred soldiers could take them prisoner without a fight.

Morgan scowled. "I see what you mean. Tell Galoone to put some men on watch."

Once the muskets and pistols were dried and primed, Morgan's crew returned to the open field. Brodely was convinced they could siege the fortress by means of the bridge—eventually. He was a stubborn man. But Morgan had no better solution.

A new wave of clouds blew in. By the time the squadrons were in position, the skies burst open, turning air into water. Cursing the weather, Morgan fired the signal anyway.

Brodely's squadron led the charge.

At best, four men could run abreast the bridge. Whipping rain blasted them, shoving them back, knocking them over the side. Others slipped and fell into the shallow moat.

Most were turned back by the continual bombardment from the corner forts. Any pirate sure-footed enough to withstand the slanting rain and musketfire, met a barrage of grapeshot. Apparently, the Spaniards had a good supply of dry powder.

A direct attack was futile. Even with canoes, they'd never reach the shore alive. Between the batteries encircling the lesser island and the manned forts atop the walls, the fortress was impossible to breach. Cursing, Morgan ordered a retreat.

Astoundingly, no one was killed.

Back in the woods, the crew broke off fronds, limbs and bramble to construct shelters for their arms, saving them from further water damage. Once the ammunition and guns were

L.L. Donahue

protected, they sought shelter for themselves. Morgan and his squadron leaders sheltered in what remained of a stone and timber storehouse.

Hard-faced as ever, Collier said, "There's talk of deserting, Henry."

"Shoot the first man who tries," Brodely suggested.

"Don't do it," Exquemelin said. "I haven't enough catgut as it is to waste it patching up cowards."

They all made fine arguments, but Morgan was inclined to take Brodely's advice. Though perhaps it was just his own discomfort talking. Wearing a coat, he wasn't as cold, but he was every bit as hungry.

The rain lightened to a patter. Nearby, a round of shots were fired. Shortly after, a band of buccaneers dragged back a horse carcass that stank to High Heaven. More oozing sores than hair covered the bony, sway-backed beast. Yet every man fought for a meager strip of the rancid, roasted meat.

Morgan figured to last another day before hunger wore him down. His girth was, at times, a blessing. More'n a few enemies had underestimated his strength and agility based on his paunch.

Rather gentlemanly, Exquemelin cut his chunk of horseflesh into bite-sized morsels. His lips curled back, avoiding the near-fetid meat. "Captain Morgan, you've the luck of an Irishman."

Being Welsh, Morgan sneered at the slight. Then Exquemelin grinned in jest. "If that were true," Morgan said, "we'd be feasting inside the governor's walls by now."

Collier almost smirked, almost broke his usual, unreadable expression. "Ah, Henry, if you were cursed with an Irishman's luck, you'd be mucking out stables, locked in the tower, *or* serving as an indentured slave in the Americas."

Morgan laughed. Indeed, that was the usual luck—or curse— of the Irish, the poor, dumb bastards. Considering the ill-timed rain and his men's disgruntled state, Morgan was feeling a bit cursed. But like an Irishman, Morgan refused to quit a battle he couldn't win.

Finally, an idea struck.

"Gentlemen, it's time we run up the white flag," Morgan said.

Exquemelin's eyes bulged. "We're surrendering? I would have thought a retreat—"

"It's neither," Morgan interrupted. "Brodely, I need a couple

A Man, A Plan, (yet lacking) A Canal—Panama

of white flags and a small canoe for a message."

Morgan scrounged a piece of parchment and a quill from Exquemelin. The surgeon-barber took notes of every venture. Carefully, Morgan penned a formal message: *You and I, governor, know the eventual outcome. To wit, if within the next few hours, you have not delivered yourself and your men into my hands, I swear, I shall put your entire company, yourself included, to the sword, granting quarter to none.* He signed it, *Admiral Morgan.*

Morgan addressed the note to the governor of St. Catharine then tucked it into the canoe. A white flag flew from a stick, fitted into the hole bored into the canoe's nose.

"Gaspar," Morgan said, "take the canoe to that damnable moat, give it a shove, then await their reply."

Gaspar looked faint. "Won't the Spanish dogs shoot me?"

Morgan handed him a flag. "Not if you're waving this."

Waving the flag wildly, Gaspar waded across the soggy field and knelt on the shore. He shoved the canoe hard then sat back, all the while waving the white flag.

Shortly, the canoe returned. Gaspar plucked it from the water and delivered it whole to Morgan. A neatly folded missive, sealed with a red splotch of wax, rested inside the canoe.

The governor's reply read: *Captain Morgan, I desire two hours time, during which my officers and I will discuss your proposal. At the end of said time, I shall deliver our answer.*

Exactly as promised, when the time elapsed, two canoes flying white flags approached. Before reaching shore, a Spanish major called out, "Admiral Morgan! We bear the governor's answer. But first, we demand that you deliver two of your officers as hostages for our security."

Morgan sent Captains du Puis and Norman via the second canoe, the one rowed across by common soldiers.

The Spanish major and an ensign debarked, each wearing full dress uniform, complete with feather-crested hats, lace collars, and flared, lace-trimmed gloves.

"Do I assume correctly that you've come to discuss the terms of your governor's surrender?" Morgan asked.

"You do. Clearly, we lack sufficient forces to withstand your armada harbored in the bay. As such, the governor is resolved to deliver up the island. He has devised a plan that will assure your victory while allowing us to salvage our reputations here and at home."

"I'm listening." Though Morgan's curiosity piqued, he folded his arms to appear detached.

"We propose a mock siege, so that neither side loses any lives."

"You have my full attention." Despite his efforts to mimic Collier's unreadable expression, Morgan's brows rose. "Pray tell, how shall we go about this?"

"The governor proposes that some of your men cross the bridge at night and storm the fort St. Jerom. At the same time, send your ships 'round to the castle St. Teresa as if to attack by sea. There, you'll capture the governor, forcing him to surrender that stronghold. Next, you'll land more troops at the St. Matthew battery."

"An interesting strategy." Though Morgan had considered a larger scaled assault, he hadn't wanted to risk his ships. "But how, pray tell, does this plan ensure no losses?"

The Spanish major smiled conspiratorially. "It's simple. We both fire without bullets. To ensure both sides comply, we'll each have our best marksmen keep loaded weapons. If all is as agreed, they shoot into the air."

"And if you've deceived us," Morgan said, "my buccaneers will kill your marksmen first."

"Then we are agreed," the major said.

Morgan grinned. The plan was practical. Moreover, it was civilized. Apparently the governor was a man who understood the consequences before engaging in a pointless battle.

Even so, Spaniards could only be trusted so far. "Tell your governor, that should even one of my men suffer injury, we'll show no quarter to anyone," Morgan said.

"You have our word, admiral. Have we yours that you'll set us ashore on the mainland coast, without suffering any harm while your prisoners? And that you'll neither burn down our stores nor torture the peasants while you hold the forts?"

"Agreed. And tell your governor, he's to keep his men as a single body. Any Spaniard caught roaming free will be shot dead."

"Understood." The major extended his frilly cuffed hand.

"We have an accord," Morgan said, accepting the gesture.

As the Spanish envoy rowed across the moat, the hostages Captains du Puis and Norman were sent back. At once, Morgan

A Man, A Plan, (yet lacking) A Canal—Panama

sent Collier with word for half the fleet to sail into port and make as much noise as possible without causing any damage.

By nightfall, a thousand pirates prepared to storm the fortress and act out a battle for the benefit of those peasants taking refuge inside. When they bore witness in the Spanish court, their statements would defend their valiant, yet overwhelmed governor who'd fought hard to defend the isle.

Muskets and pistols were loaded with powder but no shot. A few marksmen carried live weapons with orders to withhold their fire, except in the event of treachery. Until events dictated otherwise, guns were for making noise and cutlasses were for naught but waving.

Buccaneers overran the bridge. Gunpowder explosions crackled in the night air and flared with orange flame. Neither bullet nor cannonball broke the water's surface. Not a man was injured, much to Exquemelin's loudly stated elation. The surgeon even joined in, waving a cutlass and screaming for blood. It was the most pirate-like behavior he'd ever exhibited.

Morgan walked boldly among the flash and empty fire with the air of a man impervious to harm. He scowled at peasants cowering in doorways and peeking out of windows. This was the making of legends.

The fortress fell as planned. Spanish prisoners were housed in the church and guards were posted. Afterwards, the crew feasted on roasted poultry and beef. They drank enough wine to float a small vessel and, in a drunken stupor, they fell asleep.

Morgan preferred to retain his wits. So he drank only reasonable amounts. He raised his goblet and said, "To you, a finer and more intelligent governor there's never been."

The governor bowed his head respectfully. "To our success."

Collier, Norman, and du Puis raised their goblets. Brodely, who studied maps removed from the governor's offices, raised a glass of water. Brodely hardly ever touched alcohol, calling it all Devil's Rum.

As Morgan tipped back his goblet, he noticed the governor staring at his hand. "I see you've noticed my ring."

"*Sí*. Natives call the stones the daughters of the Goddess Esmeralda, or sometimes, goddess eyes."

Thoughts of the cloudy-eyed crone returned. She'd warned Morgan of gods who coveted the eyes of the goddess. Thinking of the old hag sent a chill up Morgan's spine. He shrugged off

L.L. Donahue

the sensation, reminding himself he wasn't superstitious. Nonetheless, he pushed aside his goblet, blaming the wine for affecting his mind. "It was a gift from one of your own countrymen. A bribe, actually, from the president of Panama."

With a touch of disdain in his thickly-accented words, the governor said, "Your endeavor will fail. Word of your intent has been already sent to President Pérez de Guzmán."

"How do you know that?" Brodely asked.

"My intelligence comes from the governor of Cartagena."

"That, sir," Morgan said with all the confidence of a wolf to a sheep, "is my concern, not yours."

"As for your ring," the now-deposed governor said, "it has more history than you might guess."

"Pray, do tell." So as not to divulge his own keen interest, Morgan added, "If nothing else, the story will entertain Captain Collier. He considers himself an historian."

Collier nodded, half asleep. Strong spirits went straight to his head, a fact which he blamed on his lineage which he claimed boasted a few blue-bloods. That true blue-bloods couldn't hold their liquor was common knowledge. It also explained why royalty often made the worst naval officers. Often—not always.

"According to wild natives, emeralds possess strange and certain powers," the Spanish governor began.

Brodely scoffed. "Nonsense. They're only gemstones, a bit of flash for decoration."

"Only?" The governor scoffed. "These are truly *exceptional* gems, *sí?*"

Morgan nodded. Most emeralds found in Europe came from Egypt and were of a distinctly poorer quality than the ones set in his ring.

"According to legends," the governor continued, "conquistadors sacked the Temple of the Sun, finding a vast wealth of emeralds. After learning of an even greater temple to the Goddess Esmeralda, the conquistadors searched the jungles, wasting their lives. To this day, the Temple of Esmeralda remains hidden."

"If such a temple exists," Morgan said, "I'll find it. When I do, it would please me to send you and your wife a gift of emeralds as my thanks for your cooperation. If all my enemies were as thoughtful and wise, there would be much less

A Man, A Plan, (yet lacking) A Canal—Panama

bloodshed."

Brodely held up a map. "Tough luck, Henry. There's no such temple marked."

Collier raised his head from the table and laughed. "Who needs a temple? We're going to sack Panama!"

"A final toast," Morgan said. "To the City of Panama and President Don Juan Pérez de Guzmán—may we soon meet." Morgan threw back the last of his wine, wondering if his ring bore stones from the famed, ransacked Temple of the Sun.

Exquemelin, who reveled in keeping accurate records, reported the capture of four hundred and fifty prisoners. "Of them," he elaborated, "one hundred ninety men come from the garrison. There are forty married couples, forty-three children, thirty-one slaves ... "

While Exquemelin droned on, Morgan looked out the window, watching his crew stagger about the compound. Perhaps Brodely had a point about not indulging in spirits. Fortunately, the prisoners were locked up in sheep pens.

"...and eight convicts," Exquemelin finally finished.

"Who will be here presently," Brodely said. "I took the liberty of sending Gaspar for them."

"Good man" Morgan turned away from the window. "How goes securing the base?"

Brodely snapped to attention. "From the fort defending the bridge, we confiscated eight cannons, firing balls of twelve, eight and six pounds, and one hundred twenty muskets along with gunpowder, bullets, and fuses."

As soon as Brodely rattled off numbers, Exquemelin began scribbling more notes.

"At the second fort," Brodely continued, "we found three eight-pounders. The castle St. Teresa is equipped with twenty cannons, firing balls of twelve, eight and six pounds, one hundred ninety muskets together with grenades, gunpowder, shot and fuses. In my opinion, that's the most defensible fort. It's built of stone and mortar with double thick walls and is surrounded by a dry moat a good twenty feet deep."

A rictus grin split Brodely's face. "Now for the best discovery. Buccaneers found a magazine holding more'n thirty thousand pounds of gunpowder among other munitions."

Morgan felt his luck returning.

L.L. Donahue

The door to the governor's offices creaked open. Gaspar led in eight filthy convicts, chained together. Bloody strips of cloth wrapped their feet. The stench of sweat and urine oozed from them. Though their shoulders sagged and they dragged their feet, an ill-tempered fire burned in their eyes.

"Who, amongst you, knows the way to Panama?" Morgan asked.

Three convicts straggled forward, two New World savages and one half-breed, his features a mix of African and native savage descent. Dried blood speckled the half-breed's face and oily grime matted his hair.

"Today is your lucky day," Morgan said. "Gaspar, unchain these three. Escort the rest back to the pens."

"I don't recommend entertaining thoughts of escape," Brodely said, holding a pistol on them.

Morgan poured a glass of wine and swirled his drink, watching the dregs. "Serve me well and your freedom is assured."

The half-breed spoke up. "Freedom always has a price. What do you want for it?"

"Guides." Morgan sipped the dark, woodsy wine. "To lead me across the Panama isthmus."

"We show you the way to Panama City in exchange for our freedom?" the half-breed asked.

"If freedom is all you want." Morgan drew a longer sip of wine. "You're welcome to join my crew."

"Why exchange one slavery for another? Or prison for the gallows?" Only the half-breed spoke. For one born into slavery, he spoke well.

"What's your name?" Morgan asked.

"Ajamu."

Morgan finished his wine. "Ajamu, I'm making the best offer you're likely to get."

"If I"—he swept his hands towards his silent partners—"we refuse, what then?"

"I might hand you over to your Spanish masters. Most likely, I'd kill one of your companions, then ask again. Or, if the mood struck me, I might execute you all, thus saving Spain the trouble, and find guides elsewhere."

"And if we join you?" Ajamu asked.

"You'll earn a share of the booty and when we drop anchor

A Man, A Plan, (yet lacking) A Canal—Panama

off of Jamaica, you'll walk the streets of Port Royal as free and wealthy men." Eying the Indian savages, whose expressions betrayed nothing, Morgan added, "Or, I can set you ashore wherever you choose."

The half-breed Ajamu shrugged. "We've no home anymore."

A wicked gleam lit Brodely's eyes. "Tell me, Ajamu, did you deserve prison?"

Morgan arched his eyebrows. While a fair question, he hadn't realized that Brodely cared.

The half-breed snarled. "No."

Convicts, like most pirates, were notorious liars. Even so, Morgan shrugged then drawled, "Then I'd say you're due some bit of good fortune. Have I your loyalty?"

Ajamu grunted. "You have my oath."

"And theirs?" Morgan asked.

Ajamu shook his meaty fist at the Indians and threatened, "You'll serve this pirate or I'll burn you alive."

The two winced and drew backwards, but nodded.

"Yea, captain. You've their word. But I suggest you beat them regularly into submission, or else they won't respect you."

Morgan stroked his moustache and studied the cowed Indians. To him it seemed Ajamu would better benefit from a solid beating. Morgan waved towards the door. "Brodely, show them their quarters and have Gaspar show them the ropes." To Ajamu, Morgan added, "In my crew, every man pulls his weight."

Brodely escorted the convicts out, taking their stink with him. In time, the sea air would purge them of their earthy odor.

Exquemelin pursed his lips.

"What?" Morgan asked. Sometimes, the surgeon could be a bit touchy. "You're not bothered by my last comment, are you? You've duties enough as surgeon."

Exquemelin blinked. "No, sir. But, in going over the governor's books, I ran across the prison records. As such, I took the liberty of perusing each convicts' charges."

"And?" Morgan rolled his hand, wishing he could pull information from his surgeon as efficiently as Exquemelin extracted a rotten tooth.

"Ajamu has committed numerous murders, rapes and robberies. The Indians were his unwitting accomplices, coerced into obedience. However, they were born in the Spanish dominions and should be well-acquainted with the roads and jungles."

"Indeed? The Indians may prove the more useful."

"What of Ajamu?" Exquemelin asked.

"He'll ensure they obey." To Exquemelin's still disturbed, wide-eyed stare, Morgan laughed. "Come now, surgeon. We've worse men amongst us. What's another murderer or three?"

However Ajamu was right about one thing; he hadn't deserved imprisonment. Under Spanish law, he should have been broken alive on the wheel. But that was the past. Once he signed the articles, he was a brethren of the coast. Should Ajamu steal from his brethren, he would find pirate justice swifter and decidedly more unpleasant.

A Man, A Plan, (yet lacking) A Canal—Panama

Chapter Three

The Castillo San Lorenzo

"**I'm counting on you,** Joseph." Morgan clasped Brodely's elbow as they shook hands. "Will five ships be enough?"

"I'm sure to have four too many"—Brodely flashed a toothy grin—"but I rather like having the reinforcements."

"If Ajamu or the Indians give you any trouble—"

"I know, Henry, wallop them soundly."

Morgan grinned. Knowing Brodely, he'd start the voyage by giving them a thrashing on account.

"I may lack your luck, Henry, but I'll secure the fortress before your arrival. I'll even arrange a feast."

"I'll bring wine."

With that, Morgan dispatched four twelve-and-sixteen-gunships along with a three-masted barque under the command of Captain Brodely to capture the fortress at the mouth of the Rio Chagres.

In the meanwhile, Morgan's remaining crew made the Isle of St. Catharine a safe harbor. They cast the forts' ordnance into the water for later retrieval. Eight of the ten batteries were abandoned, their guns spiked and the gun-carriages burnt. And they burned the buildings, with the exceptions of St. Teresa, the most defensible fort, and St. Jerom, the one guarding the bridge.

The ex-governor watched fire raze his home and offices. Wringing his hands, he said quietly, "We agreed, no burning."

"Would your king believe we'd leave the fortress intact?" Morgan asked.

"I suppose not." The ex-governor sighed.

"For your sake," Morgan said, "I hope your king is grateful that you survived."

"As do I."

Four days later, Morgan's fleet set sail for Rio Chagres—taking the prisoners, as promised, to the mainland of the Spanish New World.

A Man, A Plan, (yet lacking) A Canal—Panama

"Hail and good spirits 1671. May the New Year be as favorable as those past." Leaning against the ship's railing, Morgan raised a gem-encrusted goblet filled with spiced wine.

"Here's to you, my Caribbean. You're a damned fine mistress, better than any a man ever deserved." Morgan poured the wine into the frothy sea. "I don't know why you haven't drowned us all." Then he tossed the goblet overboard.

"A sacrifice to Davy Jones?" Exquemelin slipped up from behind. The ship's surgeon moved as silently as death—an irony considering the only cutting he did was to save a man's skin and not separate him from it.

Morgan spat over the railing. "That sea-devil? Nay. 'Twas a gift to our gracious hostess who carries us upon her waters."

"You are a romantic, no matter what the posts report." Exquemelin leaned his elbows on the railing.

Morgan sniffed haughtily. The posts called him a pirate. Yet those bloody chroniclers wouldn't know the difference between a pirate and a privateer if faced with the business end of a cutlass. "And you are a general pain in the arse—but you've an even hand at stitching."

"Don't forget my accounting skills and honest accuracy."

"And your modesty." Morgan clapped the surgeon's back.

"Do you think the president still has your pistol?"

"Most assuredly. I look forward to meeting him and reclaiming my pistol, as promised."

After Morgan had plundered Maracaibo, Pérez de Guzmán sent a message, asking what weapon had enabled Morgan to sack so great a city without firing a cannon. Morgan, feeling generous, obliged the president by sending a pistol and bullets as a loan.

In return, Panama's president sent Morgan the emerald rosette ring, the one which foretold his fame—if a half-blind, crazy crone could be believed. *Beware the gods who covet the eyes of the goddess.*

"As I recall," Exquemelin said, "you promised to return after a twelvemonth. It's been twice that."

"Yes, well, better late than never."

"They say the City of Panama cannot be taken."

"*They* don't know me."

From the rigging, a cry erupted, "Land ho!" The watchman pointed at an earthy streak between the deep blue ocean and

L.L. Donahue

the pale blue sky. "It's the mouth of the Chagres River, captain!"

Morgan smoothed his moustache. His venture was right on schedule.

Castillo San Lorenzo stood atop a ridge overlooking the bay. A tower defended the river mouth. Hugging barren cliffs, two more batteries defended the riverbank. The precipice along the southern side was too steep to climb, making an attack by that route impossible. Four bastions faced landward, while two more commanded the seaward side. As impregnable as the castle appeared, the Union Jack flew above its walls, proving otherwise.

"And Joseph says he's not lucky." Loudly, Morgan proclaimed, "Tonight, we feast and celebrate Captain Brodely's amazing success."

Exquemelin climbed out of the hold, clutching a wooden chest containing medicine and surgical paraphernalia.

"Expecting wounded?" Morgan asked.

Exquemelin, a far-too-serious fellow at times, nodded sternly. "Always, captain."

The wind howled, *Morgan.*

A chill gripped Morgan's spine. Again, he heard his name carried on a gust. He cursed himself a superstitious fool. Yet the wind still howled, *Morgan.*

Cold wind swirled across the deck. It blew crosswise then upwards. Sails fell slack then snapped so taut that seams tore. Morgan spun about, tracking the disturbing flutter and shift of the sails. Another sail floundered before regaining a hold on the weird and unnatural wind.

Clouds suddenly appeared, billowing and twisting. They reached downwards and sucked water from the sea. The darker they grew, the louder they rumbled. Howling gusts blasted from all directions. *Morgan turn back.*

Death awaits, rode on the wind. *Death and defeat.*

"Surgeon!" Morgan shouted. "Do you hear that?"

"Hear what, captain?"

"Never mind." In answer to the insistent cries, Morgan shouted, "I'll not be turned back by wind! Not when I've come all this way to take Panama City."

The crew rallied, shouting, "Victory! Panama will be ours!"

Two streams of sunlight bored through a black

A Man, A Plan, (yet lacking) A Canal—Panama

thundercloud, becoming burning eyes in a face sculpted by lightning. The cloud-face had long earlobes, a broad nose, and the anvil thunder head gave it a sloped forehead. Wispy tendrils fanned out like a feather headdress.

"Surgeon! Do you see that?" Morgan pointed upwards.

"It looks like a bad storm," Exquemelin said.

Again, Morgan muttered, "Never mind." He didn't want to look, but the strange, cloud-face held his gaze as the apparition slithered across the sky like a giant, feathered snake.

"Captain!" A loud crack followed.

Part of the ship's broken mast fell towards Morgan. He threw himself clear just before the mast crashed against the deck, dragging its rigging with it. Half a dozen ship hands leapt to untangle the flapping, torn sail while others tried in vain to furl the remaining sails.

The ship lurched, twice nearly capsizing. Exquemelin lost his footing. He dropped the medical chest and while it tumbled and skidded one way, he stumbled the other. Morgan, one hand rooted in a net of rope, caught his surgeon and hauled him towards the railing.

"Try to stay put," Morgan ordered.

Exquemelin, his complexion a sickly green, nodded. Seeing his chest plunge overboard, he turned even greener.

Morgan strutted across deck, employing a wide-balanced stance. Still, he back-stepped and staggered with every pitch and roll. "I've weathered worse," he muttered, looking for the cloud-snake. Not finding it, he chided himself for believing in mirages.

Pointing and barking, Morgan bellowed, "Haul in that sheet! Spill the wind from *that* sail first! You"—he pointed at a young, unseasoned sailor—"stop standing about slack-jawed and lend a fist. We've a ship to keep trim. And, boy, watch the running rigging—lest you find yourself hanging from the yardarm by those same ropes."

The crew hauled on the rigging and trimmed the sails. Though the pilot cranked hard on the wheel, neither rudder nor tiller responded. Morgan's flagship swung towards land as sure as a lodestone swung towards iron.

Morgan spared a glance for his fleet.

A heavily armed sloop tipped dangerously, its broken mast dragging in the water. Another ship veered off course, struck a sandbar, then toppled over. Its timbers groaned louder than thunder. Two more ships ran aground, scraping and tearing keels and hulls.

Turn back, Morgan. Leave while you can.

"Never." Anger and determination easily and always conquered superstitious fear

A gust blasted a hole through the foresail, sounding like thunder. As the shredded canvas flapped uselessly, the ship dipped low. The bow coursed through a rising wave, sending water and fish across the deck. The sea churned a frothy white, lashing at Morgan's flagship like watery tendrils trying to snare the ship and pull it under.

"Not my ship!" Morgan made his way to the pilot's station.

The weird northerly gale wrecked another ship on the reefs. A seawall of jagged rocks claimed yet another. The crack of splintering wood, a sound as loud as a forest felled all at once, drowned out the crashing waves.

Seeing no alternative, Morgan shouted, "Run her aground!"

The flagship's hull groaned and cracked as it beached, Morgan and his crew debarked in canoes and longboats. The storm's rage had little effect on shallow waters, allowing the smaller craft to navigate the choppy waves safely. From all appearances, no one appeared to have drowned.

Still the gale howled Morgan's name. The eerie cloud-face reappeared, but Morgan refused to acknowledge it.

Exquemelin climbed ashore on shaky legs. "This is hardly an auspicious beginning, captain."

Morgan growled. "Are you saying that, surgeon, because it appears no one requires your services?"

Exquemelin stammered. For a man who penned a great many pages, tallying the take from every raid, he was at a loss for words.

As such, Morgan supplied the words for him. "Surviving such queer winds with nary a man lost *is* auspicious." Morgan pointed towards the British colors riding the wind. "And we have the castle. I'd say that counts as two auspicious events to herald our arrival. Now, how say you, surgeon?"

"I stand corrected." Exquemelin doffed his hat then wrung seawater out of it. "I'm just thankful we didn't lose anybody."

Morgan slung an arm about Exquemelin's shoulders. "There's a good man." The surgeon felt thin and cold. "A stout

A Man, A Plan, (yet lacking) A Canal—Panama

drink ought to warm your bones and a feast will put some meat back on them. No doubt, Joseph's account of the battle will give you some cheer—and something to write about."

"I expect," Exquemelin said, "Captain Brodely will greatly exaggerate his own bravery."

Morgan chuckled. "Quite so." Victory was in the air—and, at this moment, victory smelled a lot like burnt thatch.

Riverbank warehouses provided munitions and supplies for ships in the harbor, as well as for the various batteries defending the shore. Between two warehouses hung another British flag, marking a nearly invisible staircase. Uneven steps, carved into the cliff, blended with natural rock formations, making them appear only shadows. It was the only obvious means to reach the fortress from sea level.

The blood drained from Exquemelin's face as he leaned backwards, looking up the steep, zigzagging path.

"Afraid of heights?" Morgan asked.

Exquemelin stood transfixed. "Not usually. However, I'm a touch queasy from the shipwreck."

Morgan scowled. "The ship was run aground, not wrecked. Her hull will be good as new once she's careened. Now come along. I'd let you wait here and lend a fist, but I'll need a surgeon on the march. So up with you."

Soaking wet, Captain Collier sloshed towards Morgan. "First a swim, then a climb. I'm getting too old for this, Henry."

"*Moi aussi.*" Antony du Puis wrung his water-soaked coattails. He stared up the open-sided staircase and let out a low whistle. "*Mon Dieu*, but it is a long way to fall."

"Then I suggest you don't," Morgan said, leading the climb.

Atop the ridge, a muddy moat encircled Castillo San Lorenzo. Palisades, filled with earth, surrounded the fortress's thick walls. Only one drawbridge allowed entrance.

As Morgan wondered how Brodely had breached such a well-defended fortress, his gaze fell upon a likely answer.

A charred hole bored through a fortress palisade, though by what means Morgan couldn't fathom. Surely Brodely's crew didn't lug a cannon up the narrow, open-sided steps. The palisades were constructed from a double row of pilings with dirt filling the space between. Once opened, dirt had spilled into the moat, creating a muddy isthmus.

"How very clever," Exquemelin said.

L.L. Donahue

Morgan shrugged. "Or lucky." Though Brodely was a keen strategist, this bore the look of an accident. No two ways about it, Brodely was a lucky bastard.

A wooden grave marker stood outside the fortress gates. Captain Joseph Brodely's name topped the list.

"I'll be damned. So much for his devil's luck." Morgan doffed his hat out of respect, as did Collier, du Puis, and Exquemelin. "I'm sorry to have lost him." Sentiment being a womanly sensibility, Morgan set his hat back firmly on his head. "Later, gents, we'll have a drink and say a prayer for him. For now, I expect if a man like Brodely could be cut down, there's sure to be others in need of medical attention."

"I hope there are supplies here," Exquemelin said. "My medical chest washed overboard."

"Speak with my ship's surgeon, if you are in want," du Puis offered.

Morgan strode across the drawbridge. Only two buildings stood intact, a storehouse at the end of the street and the stone and mortar church. Fire had razed the rest of the compound.

Captain Richard Norman approached and saluted crisply. "Acting commanding officer reporting."

"First thing you should know, Richard, is never make a report without first offering your superior a drink."

Norman led Morgan to the headquarters set up in the church and presented him with a black-jack filled with rum. Having once been chastised, Norman served Collier, du Puis, and Exquemelin as well.

"Seems like a lot of damage," Morgan said. "All of it necessary, I presume?"

"Unfortunate as it was, it became our good fortune." Norman pulled a notebook from inside his torn, bloodied jacket and presented it. "It's all in the report."

"Do save me the bother of reading it." Few men possessed legible writing, and those who did write neatly, such as Exquemelin, wrote far too much. "The high points will suffice."

"Aye, captain. Progress was slow. The Spaniards fired all manner of projectiles, including arrows of native design. Though they'd turned us back, they kept firing, wasting ammunition. An arrow struck Jeremy Sewall from behind so hard, it drove clean through him, poking out his chest."

"Sewall?" Collier mused. "Ah, I remember, big fellow. Used

A Man, A Plan, (yet lacking) A Canal—Panama

to be a farrier."

Norman nodded. "That'd be him. Though stuck and bleeding badly, ol' Jeremy wasn't done in. Nay. He pulled out the arrow, tore off a bit of his shirt, then wrapped the arrowhead with it and sprinkled it with powder. He shoved the shaft full into his musket and fired. The cloth burst into flame from the musket spark and sailed over the fort walls. It struck an outer piling and started the fire."

"Astounding," Collier said.

"Damned lucky," Morgan added.

Norman gulped his rum. "The rest we learned from prisoners. Since the arrow struck the outer pilings, those *we* could see, the Spaniards didn't know that fire was spreading from one piling to the next. Afore long, burning timbers gave way, spilling dirt. All that dirt pouring into the moat make a sort of land-bridge. If nothing else had happened, we might still be camped outside the castle walls. But the wind, which be right queer as you've well discovered, carried sparks onto thatch roofs. That's when the fire spread out of control."

"How did Joseph Brodely fall?" Morgan asked. A stray bullet, or worse, one taken in retreat, seemed an ignominious death for such a brave man.

"He died in storming across," Norman said. "Inside the walls, the enemy met us with cannon fire. A cannonball blew off both of Captain Brodely's legs. Though he wasn't long for the world, he ordered us to prop him upright so he could keep on giving orders until he bled out."

Stubborn bastard, Morgan thought in admiration. At least Brodely's demise was one a man could be proud of. Morgan raised his tankard. "To Brodely. A man of rare bravery." He drank deeply, though he preferred darker rum. A pinch of gunpowder might improve the spirit's weak flavor and give it some kick, thus making it a fitting drink for honoring a departed friend.

Norman skimmed ahead, flipping pages. "Whilst we overran the breached walls, the fire spread. To our great fortune, the fire engulfed a storehouse loaded with powder kegs. After the explosion, even the streets were ablaze. I'll say this of them Spanish dogs—they didn't stop fighting until a lucky shot killed their commander. Only then did they surrender."

"And the fire?" Morgan asked.

L.L. Donahue

"We set about putting out the flames, with aid from the prisoners."

"What of Jeremy Sewall?" Exquemelin asked.

"He died the day afore yesterday from his wound."

"In all, a glorious, and *costly* mission," Morgan said. "It appears we have luck on our side, gents, the wreckage in the bay notwithstanding."

"It wasn't lucky for Brodely," Exquemelin muttered into his oiled, leather tankard.

"It's better'n expected considering the odds," Norman said.

The church offices made an adequate headquarters. Morgan leaned back in the chair and propped his boots on an ornately carved table.

Ajamu, who'd fought like a devil according to Norman's report, shoved forwards a Spanish priest. "Padre Diego wishes to tell you something."

Judging by the padre's fidgeting, his reluctance to approach, and his battered, swollen face, Morgan doubted he *wished* to tell him anything, except, perhaps, to leave the New World—and preferably by means of a coffin.

"Have a seat, padre." Morgan indicated a charred bench against the blood-splattered, stucco wall.

Padre Diego knotted his hands in his lap, trembling. "*Señor* pirate, do not cross the isthmus. The natives do not welcome us, not Spaniards, not pirates, not any foreigners. To persist courts disaster."

"I've two thousand men. We can handle a few wild savages."

"Heed my advice, pirate captain; you are no match for the powers steeped in this strange and ancient land. These powers are far greater than a reasonable man can imagine."

Morgan scowled at continued use of "pirate," much preferring the more accurate term privateer. "Powers greater than me, when I have all of England in support? I rather doubt it."

Ajamu tossed a wood-bound book onto the carved table. "I found this in his chambers. Tell the captain what you told me." He pushed the priest hard against the table's edge.

"Show our guest some manners," Morgan admonished, swinging his boots to the floor. "He is a man of the cloth." Even if it was of a Catholic cut.

A Man, A Plan, (yet lacking) A Canal—Panama

Ajamu nodded curtly, hatred burning in his eyes. But he was once a slave then prisoner of the Spanish.

Carved images, of native design, edged the book's wooden cover. Its fibrous pages unfolded like a concertina, revealing brightly painted pictures of part-human, part-animal creatures.

"Why's this of interest to me?" Morgan asked.

Padre Diego stared at Morgan's hand.

Ajamu shook the priest. "Answer him, dog."

The padre crossed himself hastily. "*Señor*, your ring." After another shake from Ajamu, the padre flipped through the book's fan-folded pages. He pointed at the image of an emerald ring matching Morgan's.

No doubt, the design had amused Panama's president. Morgan shrugged. "So? My ring is a copy."

Padre Diego shook his head. "That ring belongs to Hurakan, the heathen god of wind and lightning—though demon is more like it. No Indian would copy *his* ring, for fear of bringing about humanity's destruction." As his finger zigzagged along squarish, squiggles and dotted designs framing the colorful images on the page, he said, "According to the text, the ring opens the gates to Xibalba—the Place of Fear. The Underworld."

"Pshaw. Even if I believed that blather," Morgan said, "it's my ring now."

Ajamu swallowed hard. "Then believe me, captain; here, the ancient gods still walk the land. If that *is* Hurakan's ring, he will want it back."

"If he asks politely, perhaps I'll return it." *Or not.* Morgan rather fancied the ring for several reasons.

Padre Diego pressed his hands in prayer. "Do not mock the heathen devils, I beg of you."

Ajamu's eyes bulged. "Wearing the god's ring can only incur his wrath and bring a curse upon your head."

"Nonsense!" Morgan roared. "Why do you, padre, a Catholic priest, believe a heathen book?"

"An Indian priest, who had converted to Catholicism, sought me in private. He feared his old gods would punish him if he kept this codex, the Popol Vuh. He begged me to take it on my travels to the temple in Chichicastenango. I accepted only to ease his distress and thought nothing more of it—until the nightmares began." Padre Diego turned to a page depicting several hideous half-human creatures. "These and worse monsters plague my dreams. I fear they won't relent until I've kept my vow."

"Sounds to me like your conscience plagues you, padre. Fortunately, mine never bothers me." Morgan laced his fingers. "You still haven't told me what any of this blather has to do with crossing the isthmus. I've no squabble with natives. My issues are with the Spanish crown."

"The natives are uncivilized. They do not ascribe to the philosophy that the enemy of my enemy is my friend. Here, we are all the enemy. And now that the ring is back on heathen soil, I fear it has already opened Xibalba and let loose its monsters."

"You're saying that those"—Morgan tapped the hideous images painted on the fibrous pages—"things inhabit the jungles? Come now, padre, we are both educated men."

"I have seen things the rational mind can neither explain nor deny." Padre Diego's finger hovered over the deformed figures. "These are the Lords of Xibalba, Hun-Came, which translates as One Death, and Vucub-Caquix, or Seven Death." He pointed out a skeletal figure adorned with bells. "He is Ah Puch, king of Metnal, the lowest and most horrible of the Mayan Nine Hells. This"—a bat-headed monster—"is Cama-Zotz."

Morgan smirked at Ajamu. "You Mayans have a lot of devils. You must all expect to go to Hell when you die."

Ajamu shrugged. "Heaven only welcomes those who meet a violent end, captain. Everyone else first fights their way through Hell."

Morgan smiled, envisioning a Heaven filled with pirates. There, the murdered, sadistic L'Olonnais would be a king among angels.

"According to savage beliefs," Padre Diego added, "If a soul defeats the gods, it ascends into the sky as a heavenly body."

Ajamu whispered, "If the gates are open, captain, the gods of Xibalba will hunt us all down."

Morgan stood and braced against the table. "Ajamu, your freedom and your very life depend upon keeping our agreement. Believe me, you'd rather be hunted by a pagan myth than by me."

"I will keep our bargain." Ajamu hung his head.

Recalling the face in the storm clouds, Morgan asked, "Padre, is there an image of Hurakan in this damnable book?"

A Man, A Plan, (yet lacking) A Canal—Panama

Nodding, the padre pointed out an ugly man with lightning bolts shooting from his eyes. "Hurakan comes from the sky realm. He is served by"—the padre tapped a series of images starting with a vulture-like creature—"the Gouger of Faces and Sudden Bloodletter." He tapped a pair of giant jaguars, adding, "And by Crunching Jaguar and Tearing Jaguar."

A feathered serpent drawn on the facing page disturbed Morgan more than he cared to admit. "What's that one?"

"Kukulcan, who reigns over the sea. Together, he and Hurakan created mankind."

The two were partners, a inconvenient fact, as Morgan would rather dismiss the padre and the book whole cloth. He sauntered towards a bottle of rum, purposefully adding some swagger to his walk. "As gentlemen of reason, padre, we know there are no such things as monsters."

The padre's face paled, making his bruises appear even more painful. "I've seen corpses carried from the jungle, their bodies shredded, wearing a look of horror like a death mask."

"A death mask, eh?" Morgan took a swig of rum. "I wager there's nothing to fear in the jungle but savages in masks."

Quietly and staring faraway, Padre Diego said, "I have seen things."

Ajamu wiped his sweaty brow. "I have seen things too, captain. When your ships approached, I saw Kukulcan in the sky. His winds wrecked your fleet."

Morgan's blood chilled. Was it possible Ajamu had truly witnessed the same mirage? Or was he lying because he feared going into the jungle?

Morgan waged his finger at both men. "Say nothing of this. I'll not have my crew scared by superstitious babble. Have I your word, or shall I take your tongues?"

Padre Diego bowed his head. "You have my word."

Ajamu nodded. "I won't say anything, captain."

"Captain," the padre said, "will you allow me to keep my word and deliver the codex as promised?"

"Padre, once I raid Panama City, I don't care where in Hell you take that damned book." Morgan grabbed the bottle of rum.

L.L. Donahue

Chapter Four
The Rio Chagres

Sloops, schooners, ketches and a galley, along with thirty-some boats and canoes traveled up the Rio Chagres. Fourteen hundred men accompanied Morgan, half aboard the boats, half marching along the river.

For two hungry days, they proceeded into the jungle. By tradition, pirates scrounged and ransacked along the way. Boats were for men and munitions.

A rank of buccaneers fired into the jungle canopy. Hundreds of squawking birds took flight. Not a one fell dead among the torn fronds and leaves raining down.

"It is no use," Antony du Puis said. "We only waste bullets firing at what we cannot see."

"Worse, every shot gives away our position," Collier added.

Morgan tightened his belt to squelch his gnawing gut. "Surgeon. What plants here appear edible?"

Exquemelin snapped, "How would I know, captain? I'm not a student of phytology."

"You know medicinal plants, don't you?"

"*Medicinal* plants, yes. If I spot anything good for a stomachache, I'll be sure to point it out. Otherwise, all I can advise is: If you see a tasty looking plant, try eating it. If it doesn't kill you, it's probably edible."

"My," Collier said, "but you're testy when you're hungry."

"It's a natural response to dying," Exquemelin snapped.

"Quit your grousing," Morgan said. "No one's ever died of hunger."

"Actually, captain—"

"Don't say it." *Snippy damn surgeon*, Morgan thought before continuing, "Starvation is what kills a man. Hunger is naught but an annoying pain in the gut—like you sometimes." Morgan stomped off.

From behind, Morgan heard Collier say, "Take cheer, surgeon. We should encounter a battery or ambuscade before long. If it comes to it, we can always eat a Spaniard."

A Man, A Plan, (yet lacking) A Canal—Panama

"*Oui*," du Puis said, "and my buccaneers will barbecue him."

Around the next bend, the river became shallow and muddy.

Morgan spat. "Damned river. Damned jungle. The whole country be damned."

Captain Robert Delander debarked from the lead ship and waded through the mud to shore. "Captain Morgan," he said, removing his hat. "Maybe we can drag the longboats and canoes through all this muck, but the ships will never get past."

"Off-load all ships and boats," Morgan ordered.

The crew unloaded every ship and boat. As Delander proposed, they dragged the smaller craft across the muddy riverbed. As much of the munitions as possible was then loaded back onto the smaller vessels. There being no choice, the five largest ships were stranded ... stranded, but not deserted.

Morgan left a squad of men to guard his ships. Taking Delander aside, Morgan said, "Keep to the ships and keep your presence quiet. No one is to land on pain of death, Robert."

Captain Delander nodded. "We'll die before surrendering."

"See to it you keep your word." Morgan hated leaving men behind. He'd left forces on St. Catharine, at Castillo San Lorenzo, and now another one hundred and sixty were stuck in the middle of the damned jungle. Perhaps he *was* cursed.

The squadrons resumed their march, hacking through the undergrowth while longboats and canoes navigated the twisting, bogged down river.

"Is it too much to ask for a little luck?" Morgan muttered.

They marched some three leagues before Morgan received an answer. A swamp edged the riverbank. The only firm ground followed a rise, creating an overland pass that veered away. According to the map, the pass and river eventually converged.

"I see," Morgan muttered. "There's to be no luck today." As the day was already long, Morgan's crew made camp, "We'll divide the forces come morning," he said to Collier, "and take two routes."

"Have I mentioned lately, Henry, how grand this venture is?" Collier asked.

Scowling, Morgan said, "Keep it up, Edward, and you can wade through the swamps with the boats."

"And ruin these fine boots?"

Despite himself, Morgan grinned.

That night, a black cloud rose up from the river. Biting gnats and blood-sucking mosquitoes swarmed the camp. By morning, angry welts covered every pirate.

By the fourth day, Morgan's forces dragged their feet and clutched at empty stomachs. Most were deathly faint.

"I warned you." Padre Diego crossed himself. "We are none welcome here. Your trail leads only to the underworld."

Morgan grunted. "It leads to Panama. If the underworld happens to lie *en route*, then I expect we'll be passing through it."

"Mark my words, *señor*, hunger and mosquitoes are but the first of many more horrible trials to come."

"I've no fear of demons." Even *if* he believed in them, Morgan considered himself as great a devil as any man could be. Nonetheless, he watched the jungle canopy, half-expecting it to part and reveal a feathered snake slithering through clouds. Then he cursed himself a fool, mad from hunger.

As the map showed, the overland trail led back to the river. Not much farther, scouts, led by John Galoone, straggled upon an entrenchment. The news fortified the men, restoring their vigor. Even Morgan no longer noticed the aches and pains of prolonged walking combined with hunger.

Two hundred buccaneers charged the battery. They clambered over earthen walls, firing muskets and pistols. Yet their shots were the only ones fired. The deserted entrenchment was already burned.

Morgan shoved his unfired pistol into his sash. Though he expected to find nothing, he ordered a full search.

Ajamu whispered, "The gods have taken the food."

Morgan scowled at him, then at Padre Diego before he could prattle on about trials and the underworld. "This isn't the work of Mayan devils, but of Spanish cowards."

Captain Collier and his rovers turned up a hundred or so empty leather satchels. Handing one to Morgan, Collier said, "Sorry, Henry, but it's better than nothing."

Exquemelin grabbed a satchel from the pile. "Surely you aren't serious."

Though Collier possessed a dry sense of humor, he was dead serious. "I've eaten worse."

"It's a leather satchel," Exquemelin argued.

"Which is made of cow-flesh," Collier said. "By all logic and

A Man, A Plan, (yet lacking) A Canal—Panama

reasoning, it should be edible."

Exquemelin shared his satchel with the padre, Gaspar, and several other buccaneers. Likewise, the rest of the satchels were divided among the crew.

They soaked the satchels in the river then beat them with rocks to make the leather pliable. They scraped off any hair then cut the bags into strips which were cooked in pots of boiling water. With the help of a great deal of water, Morgan's crew choked down their "meal."

"How's your supper, surgeon?" Morgan asked.

"It's surprising, how hunger makes most anything palatable. However, speaking as ship's surgeon, I wouldn't recommend a steady diet of boiled leather."

Choking on laughter, Collier nearly spewed out a swig of water. "I never knew you to have a sense of humor, surgeon."

"Obviously," Morgan said, "you've never seen his stitching."

"The wounds hold shut, don't they?" Exquemelin defended.

Though boiled leather sat heavy on the stomach, it didn't fill empty bellies. Nevertheless, the march resumed. In desperation, Morgan's crew scavenged on the way, chewing bark, eating leaves, grass seeds, or questionable berries—anything to sate their painful hunger.

By the fifth day, Galoone and his scouts searched a burned village, finding a grot containing a few sacks of meal and wheat, two jugs of wine, and a bushel of plantains.

To Morgan, even that meager meal was a sign his bad luck was changing for the better.

The sixth day verified their turn of fortune when Galoone's scouts discovered a barn holding a large store of maize.

Morgan drew Galoone aside. "Once we've sacked Panama City, John, remind me to award you and your scouts each ten pieces of eight." For this find had surely saved the crew from starvation and the venture from failure.

For the first time since leaving San Lorenzo, they marched on full bellies while singing John Galoone's praises. By mid-afternoon, those praises were forgotten and the grumbling resumed.

"How soon they forget," Galoone lamented.

"How true," Morgan said. "Man has always dwelled longer on defeat than victory."

L.L. Donahue

"Just as history immortalizes acts of infamy more often than saintly deeds," Galoone added.

Morgan grinned. "Aye. Had I a bottle of rum, I'd drink to our own immortal infamy."

A sound like a thousand buzzing insects ripped through the air. Primitive darts whizzed down from the foliage. The lead squadron of two hundred buccaneers dove for cover while drawing their weapons. Though they returned fire, no bodies fell from the treetops. Only Morgan's men grunted and screamed as darts struck them.

Morgan dove behind a rock. In the treetops, he spied a bronze-skinned, tattooed face. A feathered headdress adorned the savage's brow. On meeting the native's gaze, a primaeval power surged through Morgan. His body turned rigid. All feeling fled his limbs, save the heat radiating from his right index finger. Silent words reached Morgan's ears, *You were warned*.

Then the power released him.

Overhead fronds rustled. An absolute quiet settled over the jungle. Not even the normally incessant birds squawked.

"They're gone. But how?" du Puis whispered, squatting beside Morgan.

"I wish I knew," Morgan answered, his gaze still searching the foliage.

Collier pointed across the river. "Over there. I don't know how they did it."

"*C'est impossible*," du Puis muttered.

"They can't be the same Indians," Morgan said. His finger wearing the emerald ring still felt warm. "It's impossible," he whispered, repeating du Puis's sentiments.

"Perhaps it is native *sorcellerie*," du Puis said.

Morgan growled. "There'll be no talk of magic or curses."

Du Puis raised his eyebrows, "*Mon capitaine*, I made no mention of curses."

Morgan stalked off before saying anything he might regret. Finding Exquemelin, Morgan bellowed, "How bad are the injuries?"

Exquemelin looked up from the buccaneer's arm he was bandaging. "Only one fatality. Otherwise, nothing serious. Either the Indians are poor shots or they only meant to scare us."

Morgan exhaled to calm himself. "It's good news then."

A Man, A Plan, (yet lacking) A Canal—Panama

Farther upstream, Morgan ordered a halt. On this side of the river, the jungle grew too dense to hack through. Tomorrow, they'd cross the river and continue upstream along the opposite bank. With luck, they'd leave the natives far behind. For the moment, Morgan just hoped for a quiet night.

Yet no such luck prevailed. Around dusk, a man screamed.

Jumping up and down along the riverbank, Ajamu waved his arms, shouting, "*Cocodrilo de Rio!*"

Morgan and a dozen other pirates raced towards the marshy shore. Expecting natives, Morgan drew his pistol and searched the foliage. On reaching the riverbank, he skidded to a stop.

Log-sized reptiles coursed through murky water. A crewman clung to a boat, kicking one leg, fighting the pointy-snouted creature that chomped on his other leg. Where a row of teeth punctured the crewman's flesh, blood poured out, staining the murky water.

Panting, Padre Diego grabbed Morgan's sleeve. Leaning heavily, he wheezed in Spanish, "*Caimán de Aguja!*" Immediately after, he ranted, "Crocodiles, captain, the largest I've ever seen. Gigantic, unnatural monsters! They must be—"

"Don't say it." Morgan snarled. Now was not the time for a madman's ravings about Mayan gods and monsters. "I can see them for myself." Grudgingly, Morgan admitted the padre was right; they were enormous. But he refused to believe they'd been sent by primitive devil-gods.

Another river monster snaked through the water with incredible speed. Its mouth hinged wide-open. Jagged teeth snapped shut on a swimming man's arm. His scream was cut short when the reptile dragged him under.

The man clinging to a boat lost his grip and was also dragged below.

Morgan aimed and fired. His bullet glanced off the snout of a third crocodile.

"Its hide is very tough." Padre Deigo climbed onto a low tree limb. "Your bullets cannot penetrate it. The only defense is to climb higher than they can reach."

Morgan sloshed calf-deep into the river. A third man was pulled under while trying to reach the shore. A fourth, who was rowing a canoe, was pulled overboard by a croc who'd grabbed hold of the oar. *Damned idiots.*

"Stay aboard!" Morgan sloshed back to the riverbank.

L.L. Donahue

Du Puis's squadron lined up in formation, their muskets ready. "Fire into their open throats," du Puis commanded.

A cloud smelling of gunpowder spread along the river. Four crocodiles rolled belly-up. Reptilian blood oozed into the green-black water, drawing more river crocs towards the slaughter. In a frenzy, they fought over the carcasses.

From a tree limb, Padre Diego called, "Do you see that?"

Morgan followed the point of the padre's finger. Beneath a curtain of moss stood a crocodile-headed creature with a man's tattooed torso. He raised a staff, topped by a human skull, and pointed at Morgan. Then he vanished.

Buccaneers tossed ropes to the stranded crew, then hauled the smaller vessels to safety. If they'd seen the strange figure, they none gave any notice. Morgan thought of asking du Puis if he'd seen anything, but thought better of it.

Instead, he approached Padre Diego, still straddling a tree limb. "What was it?"

"A Xibalban monster sent to destroy us," the padre said.

"Then it's left the job undone."

Padre Diego stared towards the river. "The ancient gods aren't finished with us yet."

Morgan's neck tensed, fighting him as he turned to look. Another cursed black cloud of mosquitoes swarmed towards them. Morgan's skin itched in anticipation. "They're neither monsters nor gods, padre. Either would have made short work of us."

"How can you deny what your own eyes have witnessed?"

Morgan spat. "It'll take more'n mirages or costumed Indians for me to believe in Mayan demons or curses."

"Give them time," the padre said, his voice and gaze distant. "Soon enough, you'll come to believe."

"I'll tell you what I believe—I believe they're pirates trying to keep us from taking what's ours to take."

Morgan knelt along the riverbank and dipped his hand into the cool water. When no Xibalban monster reached out of its murky depths, he cupped both hands and splashed his face. Feeling the stubble covering his chin, he considered asking Exquemelin to give him a shave and reshape his drooping moustache and tufted barbiche beard.

For a blissful moment, mundane thoughts distracted him

A Man, A Plan, (yet lacking) A Canal—Panama

from the one real concern—Indians. Masked or otherwise, they waited across the river, hidden in the jungle. Given his luck so far, Morgan expected an ambush.

"The scouts are ready," Galoone said. "If there's Indians, we'll find them."

Morgan rather doubted that, judging by recent events. "Keep an eye up at all times."

"And never closed." Galoone flicked a kerchief in the air and he and his scouts were off.

"By my reckoning," Collier said, strolling towards Morgan, "we're near Cruz."

"By his reckoning and the map," du Puis said.

Having a good memory for maps, Morgan drew a quick mental image. He rubbed his chin, again noticing the stubble, and said, "I expect we'll find us a fight there."

"*Oui.* And with a bit of luck, a fat storehouse of food as reward." Du Puis rubbed his stomach; like everyone else, he'd grown leaner. Having been lanky to start, he'd soon be as gaunt as a man sentenced to starve in an iron cage.

The men cleaned their guns in anticipation of two fights, the one to take the village Cruz and the highly probable Indian attack along the way. To test the fire-locks, they discharged their guns without bullets. Sulphurous clouds drifted across the river while the near-continuous racket woke the jungle. Birds squawked, monkeys chattered, and something much larger roared.

"A jaguar." Quieter, Ajamu added, "If we are lucky."

Morgan scowled at the half-breed guide. "I'll not entertain such talk. If any ask, it *is* a jaguar."

Finding the surgeon with nothing to occupy him, Morgan sat on a rock. "Have you a razor in your chest?"

"Of course." Whether stitching wounds, pulling teeth, or trimming beards, Exquemelin prattled while he worked.

Ignoring the incessant chatter, Morgan leaned back, closed his eyes, and enjoyed the ordinary luxury of having a shave.

John Galoone returned unscathed, interrupting Morgan's moment of bliss. "Du Puis said I'd find you here."

Morgan rolled his hand to encourage a report, as talking, while a razor scraped his throat, seemed a poor idea.

"If they're out there, Henry, we didn't see them," Galoone said. "God-cursed heathens, the lot of them." He flashed one of his rare, wicked grins. "It's possible, all the racket you made scared them off. What were you thinking, Henry? You could have waited until we returned. When we heard shots, we thought we were missing all the fun."

Rubbing his smooth cheek, Morgan returned the wicked grin. "You have my word and oath as a gentleman and brethren, the very next time we're attacked, I'll be sure to shove you to the front of the lines."

"I can always count on you, Henry." As soon as Morgan stood, Galoone took his place on the rock. "Time for another?" he asked Exquemelin.

Crossing the river in shifts finished off the morning. Under the noon sun, the march resumed. At least the jungle on this side of the river was easier to hack through. And the prospect of finding a village, a fight, and food, excited the crew.

Collier's gaze never left the trees. "Why are they waiting? Surely they're out there."

"Maybe John was right," Exquemelin said. "Maybe the musket fire scared them off."

Collier maintained his vigilant watch. "That's doubtful."

Silently, Morgan agreed. Absently, he rubbed the emerald ring, recalling the queer-warmth it had radiated. Then he chided himself a superstitious fool. All he knew with certainty was that natives and exceptionally large crocodiles had attacked—both of which were of natural creation.

"I require more proof," Morgan muttered.

"How's that?" Collier asked.

"Proof we've scared off the natives," Morgan lied.

Around midday, Ajamu pointed towards smoke rising above the treetops. "Cruz is the highest navigable point upriver. Boats can't go any farther. All goods transported between Cruz and Panama City travel by pack mule."

"I'd expected as much," Morgan said.

With Cruz just ahead, the march moved faster. Before long, Morgan's forces reached the edge of the jungle and stood in the streets of Cruz.

Like the batteries and villages before, Cruz lay in burnt ruins. Any livestock had been run off. Only a few stray dogs remained, which the buccaneers shot and barbecued.

Like a plague of ship rats, the crew scavenged every niche of the village. Only the royal warehouse stood untouched. In it,

A Man, A Plan, (yet lacking) A Canal—Panama

Galoone and Collier uncovered sixteen jars of Peruvian wine and a large store of bread.

"Imagine that," Galoone said, hefting up a sack of bread, "they love their king so much, they wouldn't burn his warehouse."

"Or maybe, they fear him that much," Collier said.

"It matters not the reason," Morgan said, tearing into a loaf of bread. Holding the hard, dried chunk high, he said, "To Spain's king."

"To Phillip!" Galoone and Collier chorused.

The crew fell upon the wine, bread, and dog meat as though it were manna from Heaven. Afterwards, to a man, they doubled over, groaning. The lucky few retched up what they'd eaten.

Morgan's stomach knotted. Movement sent a tidal wave of sickness coursing upwards. Carefully, he rolled onto his side and opened one eye.

Slumped over a rock, Gaspar muttered, "Spanish dogs poisoned the food."

Du Puis crawled on hands and knees, saying, "The food I can forgive—but to poison wine. That is unpardonable."

"I'd agree," Gaspar said, "but it *was* Spanish swill. Had they poisoned French wine, they'd surely rot in Hell."

Holding his stomach, Morgan staggered towards Exquemelin, who leaned against a tree. Morgan grabbed a low limb and lowered himself to the ground.

"Can you cure poison?" Every breath doubled Morgan's pain until he thought he might keel over.

Exquemelin swallowed hard, his complexion green. "We weren't poisoned. This, captain, is the effect of gorging ourselves after malnutrition."

Morgan kneaded his gut. "I suppose that's good news."

Those who could slept off the sickness. The rest suffered bouts of runny bowels, vomiting, or both.

L.L. Donahue

Chapter Five
The Continental Divide

Morgan stationed a hundred of his weakest men at Cruz to guard the stranded boats and canoes. From here onwards, a mule path led through marshy plains and jungles, growing steeper as it climbed into the mountains.

Morgan drew du Puis aside, saying, "Antony, take two hundred of your best buccaneers and join John's scouts in the vanguard."

Du Puis eyes darted from side to side. "I dislike this terrain. An ambuscade could hide anywhere."

"Precisely. If I were president of Panama, I'd set a few traps."

The trail snaked up the mountainside into a dense jungle where trees grew astoundingly tall and straight. If the trees were of hardwood, they'd make fine masts. Morgan wondered how the repairs on his ships were going, back in San Lorenzo.

"It's too noisy," Exquemelin said.

Indeed, this part of the jungle seemed populated by even more birds and monkeys. Besides their squawking and chattering ruckus, a distant waterfall sounded like a continuous roll of thunder.

"Indians could sneak up on us and we'd never hear them," the surgeon finished, "until their darts and arrows—"

"Indians!" The vanguard rushed back, led by Galoone, du Puis and Ajamu. Buccaneers fired randomly into the trees. "Indians!" they repeated, their voices echoing hauntingly in the jungle.

A barrage of arrows and darts rained down as thick as hail. Cries and curses erupted. A dozen men fell with arrows sticking out of them. Most who were struck staggered and stumbled for cover.

Tattooed natives swung down on vines. A pair grabbed a pirate and carried him off, moving with the speed and agility of monkeys. Then the jungle fell quiet, except for the drumming of the distant waterfall.

Morgan growled. "What happened?"

A Man, A Plan, (yet lacking) A Canal—Panama

"They came out of nowhere," Galoone said, "and captured two scouts. We took numerous injuries, but few casualties."

Exquemelin crept closer. "Captain Galoone, what of Gaspar?"

"They took him."

"What will happen to him?" Exquemelin asked.

Ajamu stared upwards. "He will be sacrificed." He lowered his gaze to meet Morgan's. "As will more of your men."

"How barbaric," Exquemelin whispered.

Morgan ground his back teeth. "Surgeon, tend the wounded. I want to be moving before the Indians return."

Ajamu nodded. "It is a good plan. They won't follow us across the Continental Divide."

"While that's good news," Galoone said, "we're still hours away at best."

"Organize the men so we can be ready to move," Morgan said.

The march was quiet. Morgan felt his crew's ill-ease; it had the air of mutiny about it. And that, more so than the Indians, annoyed him.

In a clearing stood three stepped pyramids. The tallest one stood about twice a man's height. Hideous, carved faces stared out of each stone block. The three captured men were displayed on the three flat-topped, pyramidal altars.

"Sacrificial shrines," Ajamu said.

Exquemelin ran to the nearest pyramid and climbed its tiers of steps. Blood stained the sides of the stone altar. Bits of skin clung to the carved faces' teeth, as though they were eating human flesh.

"There's nothing you can do for him, surgeon," Morgan said.

A faint gurgling came from the second shrine. Morgan followed the noise, doubting his ears. Then he heard a weak groan, like a death rattle. Morgan climbed the steps, thinking only to put the poor wretch out of his misery.

Gaspar's gaping mouth was fixed in a silent, horrid scream. His eye sockets were empty. A bloody, ragged hole was where his heart should be. His entrails hung out. Hundreds of cuts sliced his torso and limbs. He couldn't have made the noise.

Poor bastard. Gaspar seemed fated to die by the hands of savages, like his former captain, the buccaneer L'Olonnais.

From a pouch, Morgan dug out two coins for Gaspar's eye

sockets. As his hand hovered over Gaspar's face, bloody fingers grabbed Morgan's wrist.

Fear constricted Morgan's throat, allowing only a hoarse whisper to escape. "Gaspar?"

A foreign voice issued from Gaspar's lips. "You were warned, Morgan of Wales. Return what is ours and leave."

Morgan stared at his ring, his wrist locked in Gaspar's grasp. The emeralds sparkled as though green fire burned within them. "If you want it back—"

Morgan reconsidered. What powers did these Mayan devils truly wield? Thus far, Indians proved a greater threat—and that would end once they crossed the Continental Divide. Though a dead man speaking was a good trick, any good charlatan could manage it. Morgan yanked his wrist free.

"It's mine now," he said. "If you want it, you'll have to take it." Under his breath he muttered, "You pirates."

Morgan climbed down. He laid a hand on Exquemelin's shoulder and shook his head. "I'm sorry. Gaspar is dead. I know you liked that Frenchman."

Morgan then rolled his eyes skywards and sent a wordless warning. *Leave my crew be, or I'll not only ransack Panama City, I'll find that emerald temple and pillage it as well.*

After burying the sacrificed men and piling stones on their graves, the march resumed. Morgan missed the continual grousing, preferring it over the quiet fear spreading through his crew like a disease. Moreover, he hated the ill-ease creeping through his own innards.

Jungle fronds rustled wildly as the sound of flapping wings rose like a tempest. Countless long-tailed birds took flight. Suddenly, every eye watched for Indians.

Padre Diego walked alongside Morgan. "They're near."

Morgan scowled, knowing the padre wasn't referring to Indians.

Hundreds of arrows and darts whistled through the air, fired from an unseen enemy. Morgan fired his pistol at random. An Indian fell dead from the foliage.

Morgan smirked at the dead native. "Tell your makers, Henry Morgan fears no man, monster, nor devil-god. Have them send their worst."

Indians dropped from the trees, armed with clubs and stone-axes. They attacked, screaming like the savages they were.

A Man, A Plan, (yet lacking) A Canal—Panama

Morgan fired, felling another. Musket fire cracked in rapid succession. In trained regimental fashion, buccaneers knelt and stood in ranks as they fired, reloaded, and fired again.

Indians fell on all sides. Others fled, dripping blood. A potbellied man in a feathered collar and headdress raised his spear. As he chanted, his Indian warriors fought more frenzied. Then he charged, wielding his spear like a lance.

Ajamu, armed with a cutlass, crouched beside Morgan. "He is their chief," Ajamu said. "Jaguar's spirit resides inside him. He must not be allowed to release the spirit."

"What the devil does that mean?" Collier asked. Without waiting for an answer, he fired a shot.

Blood burst from the chief's shoulder. Yet he kept charging, apparently oblivious to his injury.

"Once released," Ajamu shouted, "the man becomes the beast."

"Nonsense." Collier stepped into the chief's path and drew careful aim. His pistol misfired. He tossed it aside.

The chief jabbed his spear towards Collier's gut.

Collier sidestepped and grabbed the spear's shaft. The two wrestled over the spear. All the while, blood sluiced down the native's chest. Then the chief howled in a truly primaeval fashion.

It chilled Morgan's blood. No man could make such an inhuman noise.

An Indian charged, screaming in native blather. Ajamu screamed back and blocked the Indian's club with his cutlass.

Morgan shot the Indian, ending their argument.

Collier held the spear. The chief was hunched over, his skin darker and more hirsute. Fangs hung over black lips and his nose and jaw had elongated into a snout.

Ajamu shouted, "Kill him before he transforms completely."

Collier gutted the chief with the spear. He yanked it free then stabbed him again. "Really, Ajamu," Collier said, "I don't know what you're talking about half the time."

With the chief's death, the Indians retreated.

An ordinary, potbellied man with grey-streaked hair lay dead at Collier's feet. No muzzle, no fangs, no fur. Morgan rubbed his eyes, already disbelieving what he'd imagined he'd seen.

Exquemelin reported, "Astoundingly, captain, there's only

eight dead and ten wounded."

"Then see to your patients, surgeon." Morgan's attention never left the chief's corpse.

"I saw it too," Padre Diego whispered.

"Verily? Tell me exactly what you saw." *What we saw.*

The padre's description matched what Morgan's own eyes had witnessed. Morgen next drew Ajamu aside to solicit his version. From the way the two Indian convicts prattled on, Morgan suspected they'd also seen the chief's transformation.

"Why is it, padre, that we're the only ones who see these ultramundane happenings?"

"I believe," Diego said, "I see them because I carry the Popol Vuh, and because you, Captain Morgan, possess Hurakan's ring. As for the convicts, the pagan devils are their gods."

Ajamu glowered. "*Our gods* crossed sky and sea before man was created, before your god existed."

Before the padre could launch into a sermon, Morgan silenced him with a raised hand. "No missionary work today." He squatted beside the corpse. "Ajamu, what would we have seen, had Edward not killed him first?"

"He was becoming the jaguar, captain."

"To what benefit, seeing as only we five noticed?"

"If I may," the padre interjected. "I've read accounts of mortally injured natives fighting with incredible strength. Some theorize that these natives were intoxicated, fighting in a dreamlike state, completely oblivious. Others believe that in death throes, their humanity was stripped away, leaving only animal instincts, along with animal prowess. To your pirate crew, the chief would appear a wild man, fighting with savage ferocity. To you and I, he'd have become a jaguar."

"Too bad, then, padre. I should have liked to see that."

The corpse trembled. His rib cage cracked then split wide open. Inside the chest cavity, the chief's exposed heart began beating with life.

"Damnation." Morgan staggered to his feet. "'Tis devilry at work."

Padre Diego crossed himself and muttered a Latin prayer.

The heart swelled to the size of a bloodied head. A hideous creature pushed itself out of the corpse's rib cage like a newborn leaving the womb. Standing astride its 'birth-mother,' fleshy bat wings spread from its shoulders.

A Man, A Plan, (yet lacking) A Canal—Panama

Morgan withdrew, staring agog at the spectacle, both repulsed and fascinated. His companions retreated farther.

Father Diego whispered, "Cama-Zotz."

The convicts fell to their knees, babbling native nonsense.

The bat demon let out a mournful wail akin a banshee's cry then flew off towards the jungle, its beating wings sounding like thunder. Yet none of the crew noticed.

Morgan hurried Exquemelin and rallied the squadrons. Should Cama-Zotz return, he wanted to be long gone. If his men couldn't see the bat demon, they'd be fighting an invisible enemy.

Fortunately, battle always stirred men's blood to a fever. They marched with sanguinary vigor, eager to meet Spaniards on a field of battle, eager to take Panama City.

The mule trail cut through a narrow gorge high in the mountainous pass. Rocky slopes hemmed them in, offering countless opportunities for an ambuscade. That President Pérez de Guzmán didn't take advantage of the terrain cost him what grudging respect Morgan had for him.

That night, Mayan gods bedeviled them with cold rain.

L.L. Donahue

Chapter Six
The South Seas

Early the next morning, they crossed the Continental Divide and Morgan caught his first sight of the South Seas. A Spanish galleon and several coasting craft sailed its dark, deep waters. The City of Panama wasn't far now.

Collier pointed at the Spanish vessels, saying, "Apparently, Henry, your reputation precedes you."

Morgan scratched his throat where bug bites tormented him. Fleeing and burning down a village was one matter, but an entire city? Surely not.

Du Puis crossed his arms. "I see we shall have to give chase, *n'est pas*? I wager the best loot is sailing away."

Morgan grunted. "Let us hope they've done us the courtesy of leaving a ship behind."

Collier chuckled. "Given your relations with the president, I've no doubt he's left you a fleet."

Du Pris pointed towards the field below. "At least they left us a decent meal."

Fat cattle grazed on rolling slopes. Beyond them an orchard grew.

Morgan drew Galoone aside. "You and your men shall have to eat later. I want the area scouted first."

"Just promise to save us a good cut of beef," Galoone said.

The crew slaughtered some cattle. They hacked up the carcasses and tossed slabs of meat onto fires. His own countrymen ate like wolves, devouring the beef raw or barely cooked. A man of better breeding, Morgan ate with the buccaneer companies who roasted their beef properly.

Above the orchard tops, a steeple pierced the sky. Church bells rang. Panama City was close enough to smell.

Morgan wiped his mouth and loosened his belt.

About then, Galoone returned from his mission. "Spanish forces are laying in wait on the main road. Several ambuscades are hiding along the tree line. We couldn't get close enough to estimate their number, but saw at least fifty horses."

A Man, A Plan, (yet lacking) A Canal—Panama

"Probably a royal regiment." Morgan hadn't considered horsemen, though he should have. Spaniards were fond of the smelly beasts. "We expected a challenge, gents, and it appears we shan't be disappointed. Remind the men, there'll be no turning back."

"I'd fight you if you said otherwise." A hint of a smile cracked Collier's stoic demeanor.

Galoone raised his eyebrows. "I hope you've saved some of the beef... ."

Du Puis nodded. "But of course. It is only a shame there is no wine to go with all this fine beef."

For the first time since leaving San Castillo, the men slept comfortably on full stomachs. The next morning, they finished off the cooked beef and made ready for battle.

"If possible, I'd rather circumnavigate any ambuscades or blockades," Morgan said.

"There is a route around," Ajamu said. "The terrain is hard, but it comes out on the far side of Panama City."

Morgan clapped Ajamu's back. "Good man." He turned towards Galoone. "As always, we'll rely on you for advance information."

Galoone nodded. "If I can't send word, I'll fire a signal. Three rapid shots means we're facing capture."

Once squadrons and positions were assigned, Ajamu led them through dense woods. Hacking through undergrowth made for slow progress, but eventually they reached a rise. There, Galoone and few scouts waited.

"They know we're here," Galoone said. "They're patient, if nothing." He pointed downhill. "They're hiding on the other side of the field."

Morgan rubbed his tufted chin. "Is there a way around?"

Ajamu shook his head. "The forests grow too dense and the ground is treacherous with swamps and gorges."

Morgan drew his pistol. "It's just as well. I've been eager for an honest battle. What are we up against?"

Galoone shrugged. "A hundred horsemen and perhaps twice that in infantry. But no cannons. No great guns of any sort that we've seen."

"Sounds like it'll be a good battle," Collier said.

A scout whispered something to Galoone.

Grinning, Galoone added, "He reminds me, they've brought

their beef."

"How's that?" Morgan asked.

"They've brought two herds of wild bulls, tended by slaves."

"Could be interesting," Collier said. "Battle followed by a banquet."

"*Oui*. More fine Spanish beef," du Puis added.

From the field, Spanish soldiers cried, "*A la savana, a la savana, cornudos, perros ingleses.*" *To the open fields, you cuckolds, you English dogs*, they cried.

"As I said," Galoone repeated, "they know we're here."

"Let's not disappoint them." Morgan fired a shot, signaling the other squadron leaders. "To victory and glory," Morgan said as he, Collier, du Puis and Galoone exchanged handshakes, an old battle tradition.

Du Puis led the initial assault with two hundred buccaneer skirmishers, each armed with first rate muskets. The front rank put one knee to the ground then fired, the discharge producing a thick cloud. Another rank surged through the smoke and fired. The fusillade continued without break as rank after rank of skirmishers burst through multiple cloud banks, reloading *en route*. Even among buccaneers, these skirmishers possessed legendary skills.

Between the skirmishers' fine shooting and the Spaniard's slow moving formations, horsemen and horses fell by the score.

Morgan waved a flag, signaling his squadron to fall in behind Collier's who were already advancing on enemy infantry.

The rise was solid ground, but the field was a quagmire riddled with trenches and soggy grass. It was no wonder the horsemen advanced slowly. Every foot-sinking step stirred up clouds of biting gnats. The acrid stench of burnt sulfur mixed with the sour-grass malodor. Soon, the stench of death would overtake it all.

Morgan inhaled the noxious miasma deeply, as though breathing in life itself. His heart pounded and his eyesight sharpened. Remembering the dead chieftain, Morgan felt his own primal, predatory spirit awaken.

A Spaniard charged. Morgan fired, killing him instantly.

Pistol shot and musket fire rang out across the field. Those who'd spent their bullets wielded cutlasses.

When Morgan spent one pistol, he tossed it aside and drew another. The battlefield was no place to worry about a gun when

A Man, A Plan, (yet lacking) A Canal—Panama

there wasn't time to reload. After the battle, there would be time enough to collect discarded weapons.

With each kill, Morgan's strength renewed. The smell of blood invigorated him. He felt right with the world. Man, by his very nature, was designed to fight.

Morgan threw aside his last pistol and drew his cutlass. Not ten yards away, a Spaniard drew aim on him. Morgan charged, screaming for blood. The soldier fired, missed, then threw down his musket and ran. Morgan cut him across his cowardly backside and kept running while the man fell and wallowed in his own blood.

A growing number of dead Spaniards covered the field while surviving horsemen fled. Seeing their betters run, the Spanish infantry broke and deserted the field.

A wild halooing rose up. A sound like thunder accompanied the herd of wild bulls rampaged onto the soggy field. The drovers, Indian and African slaves, yipped and swatted the cattle with sticks. As the herd ploughed into the quagmire, their hooves sank deep. Eyes wide with fear, the bulls started lowing and slinging their heads.

Morgan's squadron joined another in the exposed rear ranks. Both squadrons charged the confused herds, waving flags, shouting and discharging weapons.

Panicked bulls clambered out of the mire, trampling the drovers. On firmer ground, the herds stampeded, running down any foot soldier in their path.

The remaining squadrons took the field. Cries of victory filled the air along with trumpet blare and the beating of drums. The battle was theirs, but Panama City had yet to fall.

According to reports, buccaneer losses were light and few were wounded. Six hundred Spaniards lay slain, their blood oozing into the quagmire. And even now countless wounded dragged themselves off to safety.

Those prisoners who wouldn't talk were shot. Finally, a captured calvary captain was brought before Morgan.

Blood soaked the Spanish grandee's sleeve. Spanish noble blood ran as thin as any blue-blood's, for he talked without the threat of torture. He betrayed the city's defenses, naming the location and strength of every gun emplacement.

Morgan looked towards the rooftops rising above the orchard. "And they say you can't be taken." Morgan smiled.

Chapter Seven
Panama City

Panama City sprawled along a stepped hillside. Only the churches, monasteries and mansions were of brick and painted stucco, their tiled roofs gleaming like treasure. The homes and shops of minor nobility, wealthy merchants and craftsmen were made of aromatic cedar. On the lowest tier, the thatched houses of the poor huddled like starved wretches awaiting a beating.

As the calvary captain had said, a redoubt guarded the main road, armed with eight brass cannons.

Using prisoners as shields, Morgan's forces overran the enclosed fort, losing more prisoners than pirates to cannon fire. Morgan then sent du Puis's buccaneers ahead, where the greatest blockades were anticipated. Collier's men took the richer district while Galoone's squadron headed towards the docks. The remaining squadrons marched through the city streets like conquerors.

At the first crossroad, Morgan's squadron ran afoul a breastwork of stacked, fifty-pound mealsacks barricading the cobbled street—just as the Spanish grandee had described.

Spaniards fired cannons and muskets. Grapeshot ripped through the front rank of buccaneers. Though many a buccaneer fell wounded, they pushed onwards, overwhelming the hastily stacked breastwork, shooting anyone in their path.

Taking one street and one battery at a time, Morgan's crew fought their way to the main market square. There, Spaniards had erected two enclosed redoubts, one boasting six guns, the other eight.

Morgan's men surged into cannon fire, grenadiers leading the way. Their successes rallied them.

A shadow crossed the land, one too dark to be caused by clouds crossing the sun. Morgan stopped. His men ran past, screaming for blood, apparently unaware of the spreading darkness.

A thundercloud swelled to incredible heights. Its anvil-head pointed towards Morgan as though the coming storm were

A Man, A Plan, (yet lacking) A Canal—Panama

aiming expressly for him.

Explosions rippled through the air. The first redoubt exploded. Corpses flew from the fort along with splintered bits of wood and sharp grains of sand from mealsacks. A few Spaniards staggered out, their clothing smoking. Then the second fort went up with an even greater fiery show.

The grenadiers cheered.

In the square, the clock tower tolled three o'clock.

The storm cloud darkened. Lightning crackled. Over the thunder, a rumbling voice demanded, *Return what is not yours.*

Morgan shook a fist. "Why should I, you heathen devils? Am I not doing you a great service?" He was ransacking a Spanish city—and the Spanish were more an enemy to the native savages than English pirates. "Am I not entitled to some small reward?"

Within the cloud's dark billows, two figures appeared—the familiar feather-crested, human-faced serpent and a giant wearing a loincloth, a feather headdress, and a frond collar. Geometric tattoos covered his body.

The cloud serpent shot downwards. As it slithered around Morgan like a boa constrictor of wind, its circling stirred Morgan's coattails. The giant bent low. Orbs of fire shot from his eyes, striking the mansions on the terraced slopes. The cedar buildings lit faster than kindling.

Morgan spit. "Damnable devils!"

Cries of "Fire!" echoed through the streets.

The cloud serpent uncoiled from around Morgan. As it slithered through the streets, a weird, howling wind gusted in its wake.

Collier raced into the market square. "The wind is picking up sparks, spreading the fire."

Morgan clenched his fist tighter. The Mayan gods could be damned; he wouldn't let a fire drive him from Panama, not after all he'd survived. His fist felt hot. The emerald ring glowed, as though lightning flashed from within its facets.

"Lead on," he said to Collier. Squinting at the storm, Morgan muttered, "I'll be dealing with you later."

Like madmen, the crew leapt after Collier. Even the Spanish prisoners rendered aid. Side by side, pirate and Spaniard threw buckets of dirt or water onto the spreading fire. They grabbed blankets or used their coats to beat down new flames as fast as they arose.

Even so, fire engulfed anything not of stone and mortar. Palm thatch burned. The air carried glowing cinders that ignited new blazes. Cedar homes torched quickly, the oils in their wood making them burn with a white-hot glow.

The battle against the wildfire lasted until midnight. Exhausted, pirates and prisoners collapsed, too tired to eat. Only stone buildings, chiefly monasteries and churches, survived intact. Fire had gutted every mansion and shop, leaving few walls standing. Whatever valuables survived, buried under ash and debris, would have to be dug out.

Morgan set up his headquarters in the city cathedral. Though he'd taken Panama City, the accomplishment felt hollow. The ruins would yield no vast treasures. Moreover, Panama's president had escaped and Morgan had rather looked forward to meeting him.

Wearily, Morgan's officers dragged their feet and took seats around the table.

Only Exquemelin was grinning. "The hospital is well-stocked." Like church buildings, the hospital was of stone. "I'm pleased to say, our wounded are recovering nicely. Any surviving the night will likely survive."

Morgan nodded, grateful for any good news. Still, he couldn't hide the disgust in his voice. "Gentlemen, organize the men to salvage the ruins. Though it's doubtful we'll recover enough to cover our expenses, it'll lessen the debt."

"*Capitaine*," du Puis said. "We may yet profit." Every officer, Morgan included, listened intently. "The galleon, *Trinidad*, sails for Peru. I am told, she carries fifteen hundred passengers and untold treasures."

Few could interrogate a prisoner as efficiently and effectively as du Puis.

The news explained the absence of women and clergy. Though the city had seven monasteries and a convent, not a monk or nun was found. No doubt, they'd all departed on the same galleon spied from the Continental Divide.

"It is my opinion," du Puis continued, "that President Pérez de Guzmán is also aboard."

Collier scratched scabs and blisters on his chin. "She can't be far ahead, captain. If we had a ship—"

"Quit scratching," Exquemelin chided, "or you'll infect it."

A Man, A Plan, (yet lacking) A Canal—Panama

Collier shrugged, but quit scratching anyway.

"We have a ship," Galoone said. "A three-masted barque was stranded in the harbor at low tide."

"Then we can catch her." As hope resurged, Morgan gripped Collier's arm. "Edward, take a crew to the harbor. The success of our venture lies on your shoulders."

"No worries, captain. Boarding ships at sea is what we do best." For a moment, Collier sounded a bit like Brodely—rest his soul.

Morgan divided the city into sectors and assigned the squadrons. It'd take days to salvage the burned out husks of buildings. Even capturing the *Trinidad* wouldn't amass the booty Morgan had promised. He stared at his emerald ring, wondering where the Temple of Esmeralda hid.

As his officers filed out of the cathedral office, du Puis lingered. "*Capitaine*, I found this on a prisoner." He presented a wax-sealed missive. On the front was scrolled Morgan's name.

Morgan took the missive. "My thanks."

He snapped the wax seal. Even before glancing at the signature, he recognized the handwriting as belonging to Don Juan Pérez de Guzmán.

As you read my words, it means you have, indeed, kept your promise of two years. Though you hold my city, you'll not have its wealth. We have escaped you and that, I hope, shall haunt you and your reputation. Know that I have sent formal complaints to the king. Morgan snorted, not caring what the Spanish king thought. Morgan served Charles II. *As you ponder your failure, look to the ring I sent you. Within it lies your destiny.* Morgan's skin prickled. The old crone had said much the same. *The ring opens the pathway to ancient gods.* She'd also spoken of angering gods. *I pray your soul endures their trials, if only so I might see your face once you are a broken man. In Panama, not all is as it seems to the rational mind. Look to your ring, if you dare, and it shall guide you to your well-deserved fate.*

The emerald ring glowed faintly. Morgan swept his hand in an arc and the glow became stronger in one direction. Morgan reread the president's words concerning the ring.

Pathway to ancient gods. The church was God's house. Even heathen Indians built temples. Was the president hinting that the ring would lead to the Temple of Esmeralda? *Then why tell me? Why give me such a treasure?* Yet the president had

58

answered that too—he wanted Morgan to endure trials set upon him by pagan monsters.

"I've endured their trials this entire journey," Morgan mumbled, crumpling the missive.

He tucked away his pistols, strapped on a cutlass, and grabbed a musket along with a baldric loaded with cartouches. Then he sought out Padre Diego and Ajamu. When he held out his hand and the ring glowed, they gasped.

Satisfied, Morgan said, "Let's see where this ring leads."

The glow led them into the jungle. There, its glow swelled, until the tree trunks reflected green light. By the time they reached a cavern entrance, the ring glowed so brightly, Morgan shielded his eyes against it.

"Caves lead to the underworld," Ajamu said.

"I expect this cave leads to a temple."

Though Morgan entered, both Padre Diego and Ajamu hesitated. As soon as Morgan stepped inside, the cavern walls grew together, sealing the opening shut, trapping him inside and his companions outside.

The ring's light bathed the cavern walls, illuminating white, glowing images that resembled the hideous, tortured figures from the Popol Vuh. Some were human in appearance; most were a mix of animal and man. The metallic scent of blood oozed from the cavern as the air thickened with the odors of death, rot, and excrement.

Morgan stifled a cough.

The glowing images writhed. A skeleton pushed free of the stone wall. Behind it followed an old woman with a hateful expression. Skulls decorated her gown. A winged serpent burst free and circled the cavern. A man with black-rimmed eyes and a scorpion tail crouched nearby. A death stag, along with several other part-animal, part-human creatures staggered forth. The ugliest of the lot had an animal snout, a diamond of black, reflective obsidian lodged in his forehead from which smoke rose, and a serpent for a leg. With each new monster issuing forth, the stench swelled, lending the air a viscous quality.

Morgan drew his pistols. He fired, not caring which target he hit. Yet the bullet passed through the man with the scorpion tail and ricocheted off the wall. *Oh, bloody Hell.*

The skeletal figure grabbed Morgan's wrist, its bony fingers

A Man, A Plan, (yet lacking) A Canal—Panama

digging into Morgan's flesh. One of the animal headed creatures plucked the gun from Morgan's grasp.

A man with black eyes, from which lightning flashed, spoke like thunder. Morgan recognized him from the storm cloud. "You are unwelcome here. Leave our land. Take nothing more from it."

"What's there to take?" Morgan snarled. "*You* burned *my* city. You've destroyed what's mine by right of force."

"You were warned," the stormy-faced demon said.

Morgan spat on the skeleton holding his wrist. "The time of primitive gods is long past. Even your priests no longer study your scriptures. Outside this cave waits a man who'll verify my words. Your own people deserted you, gave away your wealth, and have forgotten your bloodthirsty ways."

That last bit sounded a tad hypocritical and untrue, even to Morgan. In what he hoped might serve as a gesture to settle their differences, Morgan plucked the ring from his finger. "Here, you bloody pirates. Have your ring back. Will that settle our accounts?"

The monsters faded into the walls. Their glowing images faded as well, yet a whisper lingered on the air. "Do not forget Cama-Zotz. Be warned, Morgan of Wales, he waits and watches."

Then sunlight streamed into the cavern. Any proof whatsoever that the creatures or even their painted images had existed was gone. Likewise, the ring was gone, as was Morgan's favorite pistol.

"What happened?" Padre Diego asked.

Morgan scowled, flexing his hand. His wrist ached from the skeleton's grip. "The damned devils stole my ring. Stinking thieves the lot of them."

"The gods bade you to leave, did they not?" Ajamu asked.

Morgan eyed him askance. "Don't you worry about them none. We've come to terms. Once we capture the *Trinidad*, we'll leave this cursed land to the heathens and return to Jamaica as rich as kings. In England, I'll be celebrated as a hero."

After all, he *had* sacked Panama City. Even without amassing great treasure, that accomplishment was noteworthy enough.

Arrrrr....That Be All

L.L. Donahue

End Note:

Morgan never did capture the "Trinidad". On his return to Jamaica, he and Governor Modyford were summoned back to England. Unfortunately, during the raid on Panama City, England and Spain were on good terms. While Modyford was thrown into The Tower, Morgan, a man of some influence, managed to avoid a trial and prison. Instead, he was knighted then sent back to Jamaica as Lieutenant-Governor and served as judge of Jamaica's Vice-Admiralty Court which tried pirates.

A Man, A Plan, (yet lacking) A Canal—Panama

About the Author

An air-force brat, **Linda L. Donahue** grew up traveling. She has degrees in computer science, Russian studies, and a Masters in earth science education, along with a commercial instrument pilot's certification and a SCUBA certification. When not writing, she teaches tai chi and belly dance. Linda's short stories and novellas can currently be found at Yard Dog Press and soon from Fantasist Enterprises Press, Elder Signs Press, From the Asylum Press, and Carnifex Press.

She is married to Chris Donahue where they live in Texas and have rabbits, cats, and sugar gliders for pets.

From Yard Dog Press, Linda's stories are featured in: *The International House of Bubbas*, *Flush Fiction*, and *The 4 Redheads of the Apocalypse*. And coming soon: *Houston, We've Got Bubbas*, *A Man, A Plan (yet lacking) A Canal, Panama*.

From Fantasist Enterprises, in 2007, her stories can be found in: *Bash Down the Door and Slice Open the Bad Guy*, and in *Blood and Devotion*.

From Elder Signs Press, she and her husband have coauthored a story to appear in: *High Seas Cthulhu* coming out in the summer of 2007.

Coming in January 2007, she will have a story in *Loving the Undead*, an anthology published by From the Asylum Books and Press.

And coming from Carnifex Press, she'll have a story in the anthology: *Vermin*.

Her first pet article can be found in the *2007 Rabbits USA* annual.

About the Cover Artist

John Kevin Hokins (Kevin) was born on the year of 1957 in south central Oklahoma in quite close proximity to the geographical center of nowhere. Shortly thereafter he grabbed a number two pencil and a Big Chief writing tablet and started reproducing the local wildlife. That project continues to this day though the technique and tools have changed greatly. Along the way Kevin earned a degree in Fine Arts with postgraduate additions and has studied under several internationally acclaimed artists.

Though his own studies are never completed, he is an Oklahoma accredited art teacher and has taught high school art and vocational painting classes. He has also taught private classes in painting, drawing, and Photoshop in several states.

During the early eighties, Kevin was a medalic (not a misspelling) art designer with Award Design Medals, Noble, OK. While there he designed over 1,000 product lines of fashion art and a piece that headed into space on the ill-fated Challenger space shuttle expedition.

Later Kevin became associated with Realm Press, a comics publisher in Michigan, and worked there as artist and art director for their *Battle Star Galactica* and *The Drakkon Wars* licensed series.

In '90 Kevin was a quarterly winner in the *L.Ron Hubbard Illustrators of the Future* Contest and attended the Los Vegas awards presentations.

My Star Press, owned by *Star Trek* writer and *Communicator* fanzine editor Larry Nemecek, has commissioned Kevin to produce several Trek-related art pieces over the years for their many publications.

In the late '90s Kevin relocated to the heart of Hollywood and began work on a pre-syndication comic strip and discovered the emerging field of digital imaging. While there he was guest of several local conventions including LosCon, and the San Diego Comics Con.

After two more years of drawing comics, Kevin was picked up by Warner Brothers Studios and was involved with some aspect of almost every motion picture produced there between 2001 and 2006, including *The Matrix, Looney Toons–Back in Action, Last Samurai,* the first four Harry Potter films, and *Batman Begins.*

Over this period Kevin has produced several magazine and paperback book covers and taken awards at convention art shows too numerous to mention. For spare time hobbies he enjoys writing, sculpting, and being a fossil enthusiast.

Yard Dog Press Titles as of this Publication Date:

A Bubba in Time Saves None, Edited by Selina Rosen
A Man, A Plan, (yet lacking) A Canal, Panama, Linda Donahue
Adventures of the Irish Ninja, Selina Rosen
The Alamo and Zombies, Jean Stuntz
All the Marbles, Dusty Rainbolt
Almost Human, Gary Moreau
Ancient Enemy, Lee Killough
Angels of Mercy, Laura J. Underwood
Another Breath, Gary Moreau
The Anthology from Hell: Humorous Tales From WAY Down Under, Edited by Julia S. Mandala
Ard Magister, Laura J. Underwood
Assassins Inc., Phillip Drayer Duncan
Assassins Incorporated: Rehired, Phillip Drayer Duncan
Bad City, Selina Rosen & Laura J. Underwood
Bad Lands, Selina Rosen & Laura J. Underwood
Black Rage, Selina Rosen
Blackrose Avenue, Mark Shepherd
The Boat Man, Selina Rosen
Bobby's Troll, John Lance
Bride of Tranquility, Tracy S. Morris
Bruce and Roxanne from Start to Finnish, Rie Sheridan Rose
The Bubba Chronicles, Selina Rosen
Bubba Fables, Sue P. Sinor
Bubbas Of the Apocalypse, Edited by Selina Rosen
The Burden of the Crown (#3 in the Sword Masters Series), Selina Rosen
Chains of Freedom, Selina Rosen
Chains of Destruction, Selina Rosen
Chains of Redemption, Selina Rosen
Checking On Culture, Lee Killough
Chronicles of the Last War, Laura J. Underwood
Dadgum Martians Invade the Lucky Nickel Saloon, Ken Rand
Dark and Stormy Nights, Bradley H. Sinor
Deja Doo, Edited by Selina Rosen
Dracula's Lawyer, Julia S. Mandala
Dragon's Tongue, Laura J. Underwood
Escape Velocities, Brian A. Hopkins
The Essence of Stone, Beverly A. Hale
Fairy BrewHaHa at the Lucky Nickel Saloon, Ken Rand
The Fantastikon: Tales of Wonder, Robin Wayne Bailey
Fire & Ice, Selina Rosen
Flush Fiction, Volume I: Stories To Be Read In One Sitting, Edited by Selina Rosen
Flush Fiction, Volume II: Twenty Years of Letting it Go!, Edited by Selina Rosen

The Four Bubbas of the Apocalypse: Flatulence, Halitosis, Incest, and... Ned, Edited by Selina Rosen
The Four Redheads: Apocalypse Now!, Linda L. Donahue, Rhonda Eudaly, Julia S. Mandala, & Dusty Rainbolt
The Four Redheads of the Apocalypse, Linda L. Donahue, Rhonda Eudaly, Julia S. Mandala, & Dusty Rainbolt
The Four Redheads: The Wrath of Satan, Linda L. Donahue, Rhonda Eudaly, Julia S. Mandala, & Dusty Rainbolt
The Geometries of Love: Poetry by Robin Wayne Bailey
The Golems of Laramie County, Ken Rand
The Green Women, Laura J. Underwood
The Guardians, Lynn Abbey
Hammer Town, Selina Rosen
The Host Series: The Host, Fright Eater, Gang Approval, Selina Rosen
Houston, We've Got Bubbas!, Edited by Selina Rosen
How I Spent the Apocalypse, Selina Rosen
I Didn't Quite Make It to Oz, Edited by Selina Rosen
I Should Have Stayed In Oz, Edited by Selina Rosen
In the Shadows, Bradley H. Sinor
International House of Bubbas, Edited by Selina Rosen
It Came to Tranquility, Tracy S. Morris
It's the Great Bumpkin, Cletus Brown! Katherine A. Turski
Jabone's Sword (#2 in the Sword Masters Series), Selina Rosen
Judas Gene, Gary Moreau
The Killswitch Review, Steven-Elliot Altman & Diane DeKelb-Rittenhouse
The Leopard's Daughter, Lee Killough
The Lightning Horse, John Moore
The Logic of Departure, Mark W. Tiedemann
Marking the Signs and Other Tales of Mischief, Laura J. Underwood
Material Things, Selina Rosen
Medieval Misfits: Renaissance Rejects, Tracy S. Morris
Mirror Images, Susan Satterfield
Mirror, Mirror and Other Reflections, James K. Burk
More Stories That Won't Make Your Parents Hurl, Edited by Selina Rosen
My Life with Geeks and Freaks, Claudia Christian
The Necronomicrap: A Guide to Your Horooscope, Tim Frayser
Pinnacle, Gary Moreau
Playing With Secrets, Bradley H & Sue P. Sinor
Queen of Denial, Selina Rosen
Recycled, Selina Rosen
Redheads In Love, Linda L. Donahue, Rhonda Eudaly, Julia S. Mandala, & Dusty Rainbolt
Reruns, Selina Rosen
Rock 'n' Roll Universe, Ken Rand
Shadows In Green, Richard Dansky
The Spook, Tim Frayser
Stories That Won't Make Your Parents Hurl, Edited by Selina Rosen

Strange Robby, Selina Rosen
Sword Masters (#1 in the Sword Masters Series), Selina Rosen
Tales from Keltora, Laura J. Underwood
Tales of the Lucky Nickel Saloon, Second Ave., Laramie, Wyoming, U S of A, Ken Rand
Tarbox Station, Rhonda Eudaly
The Territories (#5 in the Sword Masters Series),, Selina Rosen
Texistani: Indo-Pak Food from a Texas Kitchen, Beverly A. Hale
That's All Folks, J. F. Gonzalez
Through Wyoming Eyes, Ken Rand
Tranquility, Tracy Morris
Turn Left to Tomorrow, Robin Wayne Bailey
The Twins (#4 in the Sword Masters Series),, Selina Rosen
The Undead At My Head, Ethan Nahté
Villains in Training, Julia S. Mandala and Linda L. Donahue
Wandering Lark, Laura J. Underwood
Weirdough, Inc., Selina Rosen and Sherri Dean
Wings of Morning, Katharine Eliska Kimbriel
Zombies in Oz and Other Undead Musings, Robin Wayne Bailey

Fantasy Writers Asylum (A YDP Imprint):

Blood Songs, Julia Mandala
Chaos Heir: Beholden A. D. Guzman
Death's Paladin Christopher Donahue
Gateway to Corimar, Julia Mandala & Linda L. Donahue
Spirit Poles, Julia Mandala & Linda L. Donahue
Tale of the Black Heart, Linda L. Donahue
Traitor's Gate, Linda L. Donahue & Julia Mandala

Double Dog (A YDP Imprint):

#1:
Of Stars & Shadows, Mark W. Tiedemann
This Instance of Me, Jeffrey Turner

#3:
Home Is the Hunter, James K. Burk
Farstep Station, Lazette Gifford

#4:
Sabre Dance, Melanie Fletcher
The Lunari Mask, Laura J. Underwood

#5:
House of Doors, Julia Mandala
Jaguar Moon, Linda A. Donahue

Just Cause (A YDP Imprint):

The Bitter End, Selina Rosen
Death Under the Crescent Moon, Dusty Rainbolt
Duckrt: Mystery at the Museum, Zeb Rosenzweig
Duckrt Escapes from Jail, Zeb Rosenzweig
Duckrt The Lost Story, Zeb Rosenzweig
Getting It Real, Selina Rosen
The Ghost Writer, Selina Rosen
It's Not Rocket Science: Spirituality for the Working-Class Soul, Selina Rosen
Meditations of a Hoarder, Melinda LaFevers
Not My Life, Selina Rosen
Permanent Solution to a Temporary Problem, Selina Rosen
The Pit, Selina Rosen
Plots and Protagonists: A Reference Guide for Writers, Mel. White
Vanishing Fame, Selina Rosen
Why I Blame Trump on Jesus and Other Things I Don't Dare Say Out Loud Selina Rosen
Yard Dog Color the Covers Coloring Book Brad Foster

www.ingramcontent.com/pod-product-compliance
Lightning Source LLC
Chambersburg PA
CBHW031310060426
42444CB00033B/1154